BUILDING BELONGING

A systematic approach to
school improvement and
emotional wellbeing

CATHAL LYNCH

JOHN CATT

INDEPENDENT THINKING FOR EDUCATION

First Published 2019

by John Catt Educational Ltd,
15 Riduna Park, Station Road,
Melton, Woodbridge IP12 1QT

Tel: +44 (0) 1394 389850
Email: enquiries@johncatt.com
Website: www.johncatt.com

ISBN: 978 1 912906 53 6

Set and designed by John Catt Educational Limited

For my mum Vera, my late dad Tom and my daughter Áine Rose Lynch

About the Author

Cathal Lynch has worked in a range of settings from mainstream to complex SEND and from EYFS to post-16. He was the founding headteacher of an independent social emotional and mental health (SEMH) school before becoming an executive leader across three schools as director of education and subsequently taking up the role of director of day schools for a national group of five schools. He helped co-found a mainstream MAT as the chief operating officer then – following a merger with a bigger trust – took on the role of strategic director for leadership and school improvement. He has been an Associate Education Expert for The Key for School Leaders, worked as an educational consultant and has been heavily involved in school governance as a member of an IEB and chair of several governing bodies. An original member of the WMSEND Forum, he is also actively involved in the regional Engage SEMH network.

Cathal has been invited to speaker at a range of regional and national conference and is the Education Lead for Mindful Healthcare, an online counselling service to support children who are experiencing difficulties by offering them weekly sessions, as well as engaging with their families and schools to offer advice and support.

He is a trustee of The Friends of Cotteridge Park and a committee member of Wooden Spoon West Midlands, the rugby charity for disadvantaged children. He has one daughter and lives in Bournville, Birmingham.

Contents

Acknowledgements 9

Foreword 11

Introduction: A forage into the world of SEND 13

Chapter 1: The evolution of the approach 15

Chapter 2: Adopting whole school thinking 91

Chapter 3: Prioritising professional learning and staff development .. 117

Chapter 4: Developing supportive policies and
procedures to promote consistency 137

Chapter 5: Implementing targeted programmes and responses 149

Chapter 6: Implement targeted responses and identify specialist
pathways 155

Chapter 7: Connect appropriately with approaches
to behaviour management 165

Chapter 8: In conclusion 177

Appendix 1: Teaching and learning survey 183

Appendix 2: Pupil survey 193

Appendix 3: Parent survey 197

Appendix 4: Support staff survey 201

Appendix 5: School improvement framework data overview 207

Appendix 6: National standards of excellence for headteachers 211

Appendix 7: Getting the simple things right:
Charlie Taylor's behaviour checklists 215

Appendix 8: School improvement plan on a page 219

Appendix 9: How do you feel? 221

Acknowledgements

Thank you to all the staff, pupils, parents, governors and trustees I have had the pleasure of working with over the years, especially those at CEP and Washwood Heath MATs.

All of the many local authority officers and senior leaders I have had the privilege of working with.

Thank you to Polly Mcmeechin – who left very big shoes to fill – for her faith support and wise council over the years.

Dr Helen Kendall for agreeing to support my work all those years ago and Dr Dale Bartle and Dr Julia Harvey who were the first educational psychologists to have the misfortune of having to make sense of it all.

All the therapists and psychologists who have supported my work and helped me make better sense of what I was seeing.

Ian Lowe for being professionally curious at all times, acting with moral purpose and remaining compassionate, even in the most challenging circumstances.

All the leaders who showed me how to do it and those whose who showed me how not to do it. It's hard to say which I learnt more from.

Thank you to Robin Johnson, the best cultural curator I have ever had.

My daughter Áine Rose Lynch who is a true inspiration and cover designer extraordinaire.

Julia Crook who has helped design lots of the posters featured in the book. Julia can be contacted on julia.crook@outlook.com

John Lane for being a thoughtful and reflective collaborator over the years.

Thank you to Andy Buck for his encouragement and support.

Bob, Pat and Colin at Church Leys Farm for their open-hearted generosity that taught our children so much.

And, lastly, thank you to Meena and everyone at John Catt Educational for their tireless work in preparing this book.

Foreword
by Andy Buck

Schools are a people business. Which is why *Building Belonging* is so important when it comes to creating successful schools. When adults and pupils feel they belong, that they are cared for and are healthily challenged, great schooling is always the result. This timely book from Cathal Lynch draws on the depth and breadth of his own professional journey and the ideas and successes of those he has worked with along the way. Rooted in an evidence-informed approach, always solution focused and suitable for standalone or groups of schools, this book is packed full of theory and practical resources alike.

The overall approach gives school leaders in all settings a powerful framework within which to prioritise school improvement activity, helpfully informed by the stakeholder questionnaires that give potential lines of enquiry. The approach is not to dictate how to do anything but to offer potential suggestions for what might work. It is up to leaders to use their contextual wisdom to decide which approach is the right one for their setting. To paraphrase Dylan Wiliam, 'Everything will work somewhere; nothing works everywhere; the question is what will work for us, now'.

Building Belonging is predicated on delivering structure, routine and consistency, which allows both staff and pupils to cope better with the demands of school, to lead more fulfilled and happier lives while achieving their best academically.

I hope you enjoy this book as much as I did!

Andy Buck
Founder of Leadership Matters

Introduction
A forage into the world of SEND

'You don't know me but I have heard of you…' began the call that radically changed the rest of my professional life. I was busily working as a deputy head in a deprived inner city school at this point and the caller was the proprietor of an independent SEND school, a world of which I knew precisely nothing. What was initially described as a school for autistic children turned out to be the primary annexe of an existing secondary school for children with social emotional and behavioural difficulties (now known as SEMH). The annexe was not yet built, it was to be situated an hour away from the existing provision and, unexpectedly, I was to be the founding headteacher.

At the time I was a very good classroom practitioner and had excellent relationships with the children I taught, but beyond that I had little understanding of why I was effective other than intuition and gut feeling. Coming from a mainstream background I knew next to nothing about complex SEND so – as if a first headship wasn't daunting enough – I had to get up to speed rapidly with the world of complex needs and independently run schools as well. It proved to be the best thing I had ever done and should, in my view, be compulsory for everyone serious about leading schools.

I quickly became an expert at meeting parents quite literally on their knees and at their wits end who had felt failed everywhere they had been. The families were often socially isolated, without hope or any understanding of how things could ever get better. The young people had lost any belief in themselves as capable of learning and felt totally worthless. So much so that they would give up when faced with the slightest challenge as their learnt history was that they couldn't achieve. This often manifested itself in violent outbursts that were unsafe for all concerned.

We had to reassure them all that the behaviours they exhibited up to now were happening for a reason, that they were not unusual to us and that, in reality, mainstream schools were simply not the right environment for everyone. Often it felt like the young people were washed up at our back door by the receding tides and the first thing we had to do was reassure them that everything would be OK, pick the seaweed out of their hair, dust them down and help them to straighten themselves out. We created a highly ordered, structured and routine environment that allowed them to relax into the daily routines of school and most did thrive.

It took me many years and the support of lots of insightful professionals from multiple disciplines to help me hone my understanding of school improvement by reflecting deeply on both good and bad experiences. This book is not an academic work nor has an expert in mental health written it. It is, however, written by someone with extensive experience of young people with social, emotional and mental health needs and solving complex problems to drive school improvement. This is my attempt to accelerate the learning of others and help them do things much quicker than I did by not repeating my many mistakes, thus giving them a better sense of what works and why.

This is not the finished article as it is designed to evolve over time but the broad principles will remain the same and provide a robust starting point for your school improvement journey be you a classroom practitioner, headteacher, governor, trustee, senior or middle leader, or a CEO of a multi-academy trust.

Chapter 1
The evolution of the approach

'Were those people real?'

– Year 5 pupil

When we opened the SEMH primary school we were operating in two small rooms in the existing secondary school due to building delays at the new site. We started off with seven pupils, two teachers (of which I was one) and two key workers. Very gradually, we grew the staff team as pupil numbers increased, but our class sizes remained small. Before too long our small school of 'unteachable', volatile pupils became highly successful and we began taking admissions from multiple local authorities, all looking on us as the last roll of the dice before residential placements. We were expensive, very expensive. In fact, we were more expensive than Eton, yet we were a fraction of the cost of residential provision that at the time could easily cost £250,000 a year for 52-week care.

Our first experience of Ofsted came early. Because the designation of the existing site was extending from secondary to include primary provision, we needed what is known as a 'material changes inspection', where the inspectorate come to ensure that all regulations are being adhered to and that the curriculum is fit for purpose. The inspector was very complimentary about his visit and said he couldn't think of a single improvement we could make. This gave us the confidence we needed to really begin to explore what we could do. We adopted an outward looking approach and a belief in reaching out to make friends with unusual people because we acknowledged that's when wonderful learning could happen. We did outdoor learning through forest schools, took children horse riding, had multiple curriculum-related educational visits (not trips) and created a calm, ordered and reflective environment where everyone could succeed.

In order to build a school from scratch we realised that we needed to be absolutely clear about what we stood for so we began by looking at existing good practice in our secondary school and adopting what we felt would work. We started by using the secular old school prayer that gave a neat summation for pupils, parents and staff of what we were trying to do. This was recited at the start and end of every day and new arrivals would say it by themselves once they were confident they knew it, as a sign that they now belonged in the school.

THE OLD SCHOOL PRAYER

Give me the strength and courage today and every day:
To do the things I must, even those I don't enjoy
To do as I am asked, without demanding 'Why?'
To be honest and fair in all I do and say
To consider others' needs, not just get my own way
To treat others' feelings with gentleness and grace
To look every challenge bravely in the face
To see what is right without looking to blame
To open my mind and door to change

Figure 1: The Old School Prayer

During their assessment week, prospective pupils wore the uniform of their previous school so they could demonstrate they wanted to change to make better choices. Once we were happy that we would get support from their families to achieve this, we presented them with their new school uniform that they had earned. It was a powerful symbol of success that was alien to all of them up until this point. It also made the point that they had earned the right to belong in the school.

We combined this with a clear definition of what was informing our curriculum as we knew building resilience would be key for our young people. They had learnt to fail and failed to learn at every other setting they had attended, which made them prone to giving up before they attempted to undertake an activity. We knew rebuilding their perception of themselves as learners would be key. They generally had very little experience to draw on to inform their learning so we knew we needed to immerse them in experiences in order to try to re-engage them with education.

WHAT DO WE UNDERSTAND BY CREATIVE THINKING?

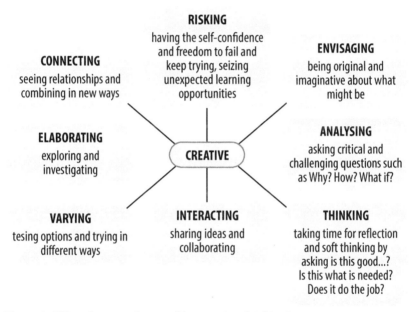

Figure 2: What do we understand by creative thinking?

We also realised that our children didn't know how to be still. I described them as like the old wobbly Rhubarb and Custard cartoons narrated by Richard Briars. They had ill-defined edges and so struggled to recalibrate their emotions because they didn't know where their edges were. We needed to help them through the use of reflection, moments of stillness and relentless structures and routines so that school became predictable and felt safe.

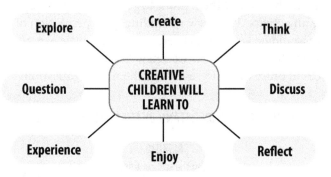

Figure 3: Our shared expectations of creative thinking

We ensured that the children were kept fully aware of any planned visitors, staffing changes and events on a weekly and daily basis. We had staff briefings every day before school and debriefings after that ensured we all understood our own and each other's responsibilities for the day. We ran through the timetable at the start of every day with the children then recapped what we had done and what we were going to do for the rest of the day at lunchtime. We finished the day by reflecting back over the whole day and looking forward to what would happen the next day so there were never any surprises that could increase anxiety.

Five keys to improvement

Part of the struggle that we observed in our young people was that they lacked the emotional vocabulary to explain their emotions. This needed a whole school solution, so we created our 'five keys to improvement' to help define our culture and inform our climate. They became the basis for every assembly, every reward and every sanction. They also formed the basis of our daily reflective journals that helped the young people know exactly what they needed to do when and served as home school diaries. They had to be signed by parents/carers every evening so that expectations of standards and behaviours were completely transparent and understood. An unsigned journal often became an early warning signal that something wasn't right at home and would lead to us making contact to see if there was anything we needed to know or could help with.

RESILIENCE (STICKABILITY)

- Learn to embrace and celebrate success in others.
- Remember that failure can be the first step on the road to success.
- Try to think positively...'I can do it'.
- Know your original shape and be able to bounce back to it when you get stretched or squashed.
- Accept that learning will cause anxiety.

Figure 4: Resilience

We talked openly about our emotions and modelled what we found hard; we needed children to understand that it was possible for more than one person to succeed at a time and that by celebrating the success of others it made us stronger collectively. Children could nominate other people for rewards when they saw them doing well but always by using the language of our keys. We talked about the 'knotty' feeling that we get in our stomach when attempting new challenges and helped them to understand the feelings they experienced were normal and not something to be feared. Anxiety became something we all talked openly about which greatly helped many of the children who thought these feelings were unique to them and, therefore, they were somehow different.

HUNGER TO ACHIEVE

- Allow yourself to dream. Aspire and visualise success.
- Still want success even after setbacks.
- Understand that others doing well doesn't lessen your achievements.
- Understand that what you have done in the past has not always worked for you.
- Remember lack of success in the past does not prevent future achievement.

Figure 5: Hunger to achieve

We talked about concepts such as visualising what a successful morning or afternoon might look like, in assembly we used videos of sports starts such as England rugby star Jonny Wilkinson mentally rehearsing his goal-kicking to show adults using the same techniques. We broke everything down in to small, manageable chunks so that children knew exactly what they needed to do in order to succeed and did not feel immediately overwhelmed at the seeming enormity of the task.

PEOPLE SKILLS

- Know that respect is like a boomerang. If you give respect to others you will get it back.
- Be a leader and not a follower.
- Be sensitive to your own needs and consider the needs of others.
- Try to not make yourself feel better at the expense of others.
- Be satisfied with your best efforts and know your best is good enough.
- Seek solutions and resolutions instead of problems and conflicts.

Figure 6: People skills

Our keys became the DNA of our school, they ran through it like letters on a stick of rock but they also evolved organically to reflect changing needs. And we didn't always get it right. We had new diaries and posters made with the statements above included and in our first week of using them I watched as one boy politely asked another something totally innocuous only to be met by a torrent of invective. It became apparent that although it might be a good aspiration, respect is not always like a boomerang. And for our children it was manifestly untrue that if they gave respect they would get it back but we were unaware of emotional transference at that point so the posters and diaries were quickly changed to remove the statement.

Lots of our keys evolved from very close observations of learners' behaviour. We noticed, for example, when someone else in a class was struggling our children could not help but seek to garner praise for themselves by proffering their work to seek validation. The effect of this however was – as on a see-saw – to push themselves up by pushing the other child down. The phrase 'are you making yourself feel good at the expense of others' became a hugely important and successful behaviour modifier that averted lots of potentially explosive incidents in the school.

Other behaviours were harder to unpick, sometimes children would allow someone else the last piece of fruit or the last pudding because they craved the instant validation of praise. Through our debriefing it eventually dawned on us that such actions would often lead to extreme behaviours, sometimes days later. We realised the short-term praise was not enough to stop some pupils from fixating on the child they had showed the kindness to and so it was counterproductive. Instead we removed debate by creating a key that insisted they were sensitive to their own needs as well as those of others which was always adequate justification and avoided future problems.

KNOWLEDGE OF LIFE AND ITS RULES

- Understand the rules and their consequences so that you can make smarter decisions.
- Know that school is a safe environment where there are people who value you and will listen when you speak.
- Know it is never too late to start again.
- Learn to accept praise graciously.
- Do not fear change, accept that it can be the start of something wonderful.
- Do not be afraid to ask for help. We all need help from time to time.

Figure 7: Knowledge of life and its rules

Our close observations also allowed deep staff reflection in our daily pre-school and end of day debriefs that were attended by all staff. A key message after challenging times was that staff must not flatter themselves by thinking any incident involving them was personal. It was purely about the child's lived experiences, something we would later understand as developmental trauma. Extreme behaviours could be triggered by a perceived unfairness or a situation, sight or sound that transported them back to negative past experiences.

We explicitly told children that by coming to our school they were going to start to do well but also that in itself would be hard because they were unused to hearing positive things about themselves. They would often sabotage their success rather than face the unfamiliar and uncomfortable feeling of succeeding.

We used the analogy of hearing praise as being like a small pebble but anything vaguely negative as being the size of a boulder. Very gradually, the children slowly started to make progress when they learnt to accept the help we were trying to give them. They still tested boundaries from time to time, sometimes just to test they were still there and that we would continue to keep them safe.

PLANNING FOR SUCCESS

- Deal with acorns before they grow into oak trees.
- Be prepared fully for the task in hand.
- Learn to expect and celebrate success.
- Be honest, set realistic, attainable goals and do your best to reach your targets.
- Be balanced and flexible and change what doesn't work for you.

Figure 8: Planning for success

Another key that proved highly effective was dealing with acorns before they grew into oak trees. There were numerous pastoral chats where imaginary acorns were thrown out of the back door before they were able to grow into mighty oak trees and risk overwhelming us. They often stuck to what they knew so we repeatedly told them they couldn't do homework all the time, nor play computer games or eat one type of food, they needed to have balance in life.

Keys became our attempt to hardwire a default setting that moved away from their impulsive actions of the past by creating a consistent calm script that adults could use. It also helped prevent what we termed 'weadling'. This was the act of attempting to play one adult off against another as any perceived slight or unfairness could have explosive consequences that we wanted children to learn to avoid.

THE FIVE KEYS TO IMPROVEMENT

SACRED HEART CATHOLIC PRIMARY SCHOOL

HUNGER TO ACHIEVE

- I know I can share my thoughts and feelings
- I know what will happen when my behaviour is good or bad
- I know working with my friends can help me more and makes me happy
- I know it is good to try new and difficult things
- I can learn from my mistakes

KNOWLEDGE OF LIFE AND ITS RULES

- I know that everyone has strengths and weaknesses
- I have people around me who will support me and keep me safe
- I know that my best is good enough
- I don't have to be worried to say what I am thinking or feeling
- I know that the choices I make will have consequences

HUNGER TO ACHIEVE

- I keep on trying even when learning gets tricky
- I can do anything I set my mind to do
- I should never be scared to ask questions about the world around me
- I know that every achievement is a reward in itself
- I am proud of my own and other people's success

GOOD COMMUNITY MEMBERSHIP

- I celebrate all of our communities
- I join in with community activities and make new friends
- I respect all members of my own and other communities
- I help people in my community
- I take care of my local area

MANAGE INFORMATION

- I know information comes from many different sources
- I can sort different pieces of information with care
- I use information responsibly
- I can present information in different ways
- I can manage information and stay safe

THINK. DID YOU ASK ANY GOOD QUESTIONS TODAY?

THE FIVE KEYS TO IMPROVEMENT

HOLBROOK PRIMARY

RESILIENCE (STICKABILITY)

- I will say I can and never I can't
- I know it's ok not to succeed the first time but will try and try again
- I expect to make mistakes, but I will enjoy getting back on track
- I know that new learning will make me feel anxious but I will give it my best shot
- Success comes from the drive to keep going

KNOWLEDGE OF LIFE AND ITS RULES

- I accept and understand the need for rules, know the consequences of my choices both for myself and for others
- I learn from every experience and have high aspirations including school and beyond
- I can adapt to the environment I am in and embrace change
- I am sensitive to my own and to the needs of others
- I am tolerant and show empathy to others and their opinions

HUNGER TO ACHIEVE

- I want to learn
- I am the driver of my own learning
- I need the confidence to believe in myself
- I will always try to face new challenges with enthusiasm
- I want to achieve my aspirations/dreams

WORKING TOGETHER

- Understand and respect different culture in our own, wider and global communities
- We value everyone's contibutions as part of the Holbrook family
- Be sensitive to your own needs and consider the needs of others
- We recognise strengths in ourselves and others and when others need support
- We understand our role within a team and carry it out with consideration of others

PATHWAYS TO SUCCESS

- I know and understand how to work hard and that a positive attiude to learning will bring success
- I understand that we all have different pathways to success
- To be successful I need to challenge myself
- I will stay focused on my goals
- I am able to celebrate the success of myself and others

THINK. DID YOU ASK ANY GOOD QUESTIONS TODAY?

Figures 9 and 10: On the two previous pages are examples of the five keys created with other schools

We began to ask our young people to predict their learning and behaviour score each day, which soon showed us that our children often had unrealistic expectations, setting themselves the target of a perfect score for the day which put them under huge pressure to perform. In fact, it often became the thing that stopped them achieving so we created a new key: remember wanting something too much can be the thing that stops you achieving it. As soon as something went wrong or a score was not earned, they became overwhelmed by disappointment and a sense of shame, often leading to meltdowns. We encouraged our young people to be happy with doing well rather than being perfect, as perfect was not sustainable.

Our keys helped support our daily reflection and we introduced the concept of a 'learn-o-meter' for children to self-assess how they thought they had been as a learner that day. We consulted children on any proposed change and when we asked what the opposite of being poor in learning terms one young man pointed out that we should use rich because all sorts of things can happen when you are a good learner. So poor and rich it became in our diaries. Another pupil asked if we could include a scale for how anxious they felt which allowed us to gain insight on how they were feeling and which keys had helped or would have helped them to succeed. We saw how much our relaxation sessions straight after lunch helped support children with key transitions and understood how the structures and routines that we had created were essential to improving outcomes.

Our daily reflective diaries helped create a highly structured assessment framework covering learning and safety. The children were encouraged to think about how they felt and use emoticons to try to express it. They could also earn one merit for each 15 minutes of good attainment as well as an overall score for each lesson/time period related to behaviour. A level three behaviour indicated that pupils had fully complied with all rules and had, therefore, kept themselves safe. (See Appendix 9)

HOW I AM FEELING	HOW HAVE YOU BEEN AS A LEARNER TODAY?	LEARNING OBJECTIVE	ATTAINMENT MERITS	SAFETY LEVEL	STAFF COMMENT
(face)	POOR 0 1 2 3 4 5 6 7 8 9 (10) RICH	Breakfast / Assembly	3 / 2	1 2 (3) Just	Listened well
(face)	POOR 0 1 2 3 4 5 6 7 8 9 (10) RICH	Journey to Taking the Reins	2 / 2	1 2 (3)	Good journey
(face)	POOR 0 1 2 3 4 5 6 7 8 (9) 10 RICH	Taking the Reins	8 / 8	1 2 (3)	Fantastic worked well with the horses
(face)	POOR 0 1 2 3 4 5 6 7 8 9 (10) RICH	Journey from Taking the Reins	2 / 2	1 2 (3)	Good journey
(face)	POOR 0 1 2 3 4 5 6 7 8 9 (10) RICH	Lunch	3 / 3	1 2 (3)	watch a game of chess appropriately without interfering. well done!
(face)	POOR 0 1 2 3 4 5 6 7 8 9 (10) RICH	Relaxation	— / —	1 2 (3)	Calm

Figure 11: Example of a reflective diary for a morning

DAY: Tuesday

DATE: 9/11/10

HOW I AM FEELING	HOW HAVE YOU BEEN AS A LEARNER TODAY?	LEARNING OBJECTIVE	ATTAINMENT MERITS	SAFETY LEVEL	STAFF COMMENT
◯	POOR 0 1 2 3 4 5 6 7 8 9 10 RICH	Topic/Art		1 2 **(3)**	KW - Chose library book witch Child by Celia Rees.
◯	POOR 0 1 2 3 4 5 6 7 8 9 10 RICH	I can sketch a drawing of an alien	$\frac{5}{5}$	1 2 3	Talked about annual review
◯	POOR 0 1 2 3 4 5 6 7 8 9 10 RICH			1 2 3	

HOW ANXIOUS HAVE I FELT TODAY?

NOT AT ALL 0 1 2 **3** 4 5 6 7 8 9 10 VERY

		TARGET SCORE	ACTUAL SCORE
COMMENDATIONS		5	6
	LEVEL	5	3

WHY? What has made me anxious?
- Going to see the horses today because I didn't know if they'd like me

HOW HAVE I BEEN AS A LEARNER TODAY?

POOR 0 1 2 3 4 5 6 7 8 9 **10** RICH

HAS ANYTHING STOPPED ME LEARNING TODAY?

no

HOW MUCH HAVE I ENJOYED SCHOOL TODAY?

NOT AT ALL 0 1 2 3 4 5 6 7 8 9 **10** VERY

WHICH OF MY 5 KEYS HELPED ME / WOULD HAVE HELPED ME IMPROVE TODAY? Be a leader not a follower
You only truly fail when you stop trying

HOMEWORK:
Use the words in sentences
Bring in newspapers

PARENT / CARER COMMENT:
no

HEAD OF LEARNING COMMENT:
A great day - good to see you used keys to cope with horse anxiety

Figure 12: The above example is of a completed day page in our reflective journal

This example (see figures 11 and 12) is from a previous school refuser who had been out of school for over a year. Note how much they enjoyed school that day (10 with lots of ++++++). They were able to articulate that going to see the horse made them anxious because they didn't know if the horse would like them and identify what keys helped them (being a leader not a follower, you only truly fail when you stop trying). We can also see that their target score was 5 for attainment and 3 for safety, rather than the maximum score of 6/3.

It took this young person (see figure 13 on the adjacent page) till the end of the day to write down why they had struggled (family argument) and which key would have helped them sooner (know that school is a safe environment where there are people who value you and will listen when you speak). However, they enjoyed school (10) and thought they had been a rich learner (10).

What we discovered was that when we presented the opportunity for reflection, although it was often uncomfortable that our children could learn to get much better through our supportive approaches. We began to be able to collect data at individual pupil level about which times, subjects or days they struggled so we could plan and support more effectively. It highlighted for us just quite how hard transitional times were for our children as anxiety ebbed and flowed depending on a range of factors that were never the same for any two children and were often different for individuals from day to day.

Our reflective journals gave us lots of additional daily intelligence such as an unrealistic target scores or poor parental engagement that could give clues to potential underlying problems and through our pre- and post-school briefings we could adapt individual provision with a truly personalised approach.

The glue that really helped hold everything together was the pastoral work undertaken by our key working team with our young people. The pupils had regular timetabled one to one sessions to make space for reflection and ensure all pupils had a consistent positive adult role model who could hold them in mind, empathise with them, support their social and emotional learning and build relationships with home.

DATE: 15/2/11
DAY: Tuesday

HOW I AM FEELING	HOW HAVE YOU BEEN AS A LEARNER TODAY?	LEARNING OBJECTIVE	ATTAINMENT MERITS	SAFETY LEVEL	STAFF COMMENT
◯	POOR 0 1 2 3 4 5 6 7 8 9 10 RICH	Relaxation	— / —	1 2 ③ / J	A little silliness. Turned it around and made good choices
◯	POOR 0 1 2 3 4 5 6 7 8 9 10 RICH	Literacy - I can read/listen and answer questions on Alice in Wonderland	5 / 5	1 2 ③	Listened well
◯	POOR 0 1 2 3 4 5 6 7 8 9 10 RICH			1 2 3	

COMMENDATIONS	LEVEL	TARGET SCORE	ACTUAL SCORE
		6	3 J

HOW ANXIOUS HAVE I FELT TODAY?
NOT AT ALL 0 1 2 ③ 4 5 6 7 8 9 10 VERY

WHY? Family arguement

HOW HAVE I BEEN AS A LEARNER TODAY?
POOR 0 1 2 3 4 5 6 7 8 9 ⑩ RICH

HAS ANYTHING STOPPED ME LEARNING TODAY? no

HOW MUCH HAVE I ENJOYED SCHOOL TODAY?
NOT AT ALL 0 1 2 3 4 5 6 7 8 9 ⑩ VERY

WHICH OF MY 5 KEYS HELPED ME / WOULD HAVE HELPED ME IMPROVE TODAY? Know that school is a safe environment where there are people who value you and will listen when you speak

HEAD OF LEARNING COMMENT: A good day today. Made good choices Sam. Well done!

PARENT/CARER COMMENT:

HOMEWORK: Silent C

Figure 13: Example of a reflective diary for an afternoon (see appendix 9 for a range of emoticons that children could choose)

29

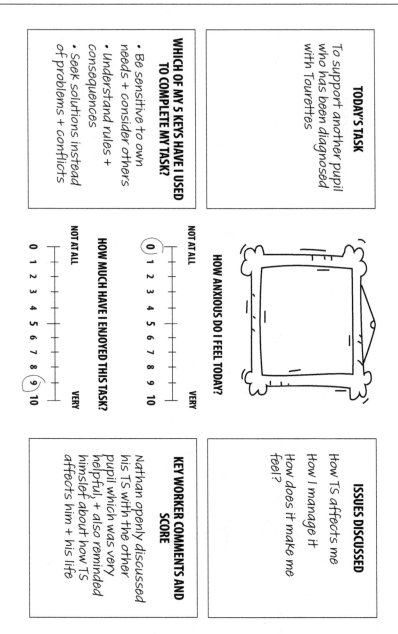

TODAY'S TASK

To support another pupil who has been diagnosed with Tourettes

WHICH OF MY 5 KEYS HAVE I USED TO COMPLETE MY TASK?

• Be sensitive to own needs + consider others
• Understand rules + consequences
• Seek solutions instead of problems + conflicts

HOW ANXIOUS DO I FEEL TODAY?

NOT AT ALL ⓪ 1 2 3 4 5 6 7 8 9 10 VERY

HOW MUCH HAVE I ENJOYED THIS TASK?

NOT AT ALL 0 1 2 3 4 5 6 7 8 ⑨ 10 VERY

ISSUES DISCUSSED

How TS affects me
How I manage it
How does it make me feel?

KEY WORKER COMMENTS AND SCORE

Nathan openly discussed his TS with the other pupil which was very helpful, + also reminded himslef about how TS affects him + his life

Figure 14: Key worker paperwork in relation to a session in which a pupil discussed the impact of his tics

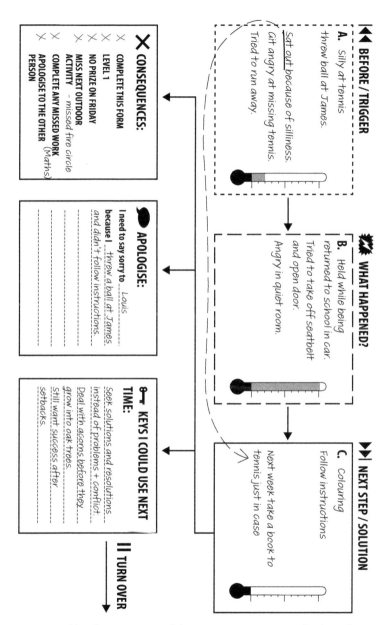

Figure 15: A self-reflection created by a young person with their key worker following a restraint breaking the incident down to aid understanding.

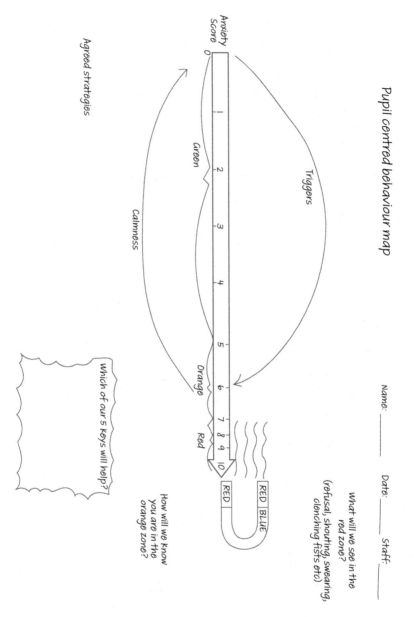

Figure 16: Above blank template of a pupil centred behaviour map focusing on anxiety

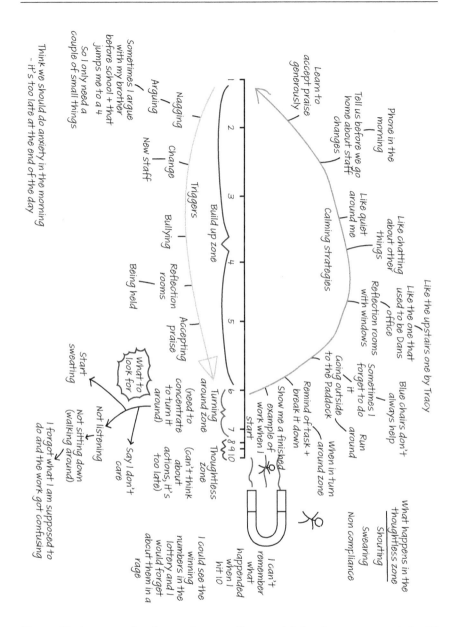

Figure 17: An example of secondary pupil centred behaviour map created with staff focusing on anxiety

By getting children to reflect on their anxiety with a trusted member of staff we always discovered things that we didn't know that could inform our behaviour plans. Children named the different zones, in this example (see figure 17) calling them the build-up zone, turn around zone and the thoughtless zone. Note that in the thoughtless zone the scale gets closer together and if they enter it there is a danger of being pulled right over the edge as if by a big magnet. The turnaround zone was where things could go either way; there was still a chance to calm down if the situation was skilfully handled by staff, but there was also a danger of things escalating.

They were able to identify what triggered anxiety (nagging, arguing, sometimes I argue with my brother before school and that jumps me to a 4 so I only need a couple of small things, changes, new staff, bullying, reflection room, being held, accepting praise), what signs staff could look out for when they entered the turning around zone (saying I don't care, sweating, not listening, walking around or not sitting down, and forgetting what they are supposed to do as the work gets too confusing) and what helps them calm (accepting praise graciously, being told in advance about staff changes including phoning home in the morning to let them know if needs be, chatting about other things, going to reflection rooms with windows so they can look outside, going outside, reminding of the task and breaking it down, showing a finished example of work before they start). They were also able to articulate what happens in the thoughtless zone (can't think about actions it's too late, shouting, swearing, non-compliance, can't remember what happened when they hit ten, I could see the winning numbers in the lottery and I would forget about them in a rage).

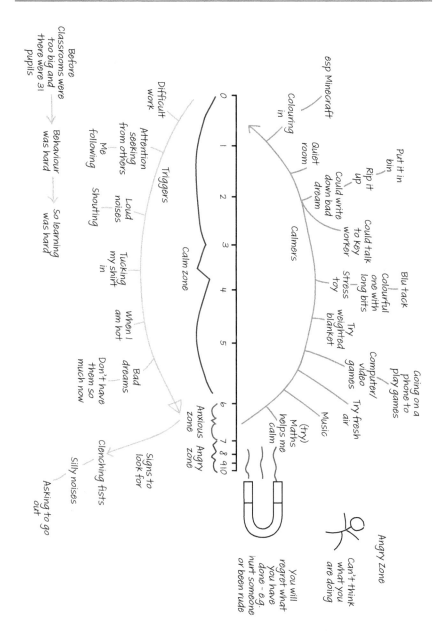

Figure 18: An example of a primary pupil centred behaviour map created with staff focusing on anxiety

In figure 18 you will see the zones named as calm zone, anxious zone and angry zone. Triggers included difficult work, attention seeking from others and me following, loud noises/shouting, tucking my shirt in, being hot and bad dreams. Things that helped calming included Minecraft, colouring in, writing down a bad dream, ripping it up and putting it in the bin, talking to key worker, using stress toys/blu-tack, a weighted blanket, computer games, fresh air, music and maths. Signs of entering the anxious zone were clenched fists, making silly noises and asking to go outside. Once the angry zone had been breached you can't think what you are doing and you will regret what you have done, e.g. hurting someone or being rude. In other words you will feel shame.

It is worth saying that drawing these rudimental diagrams was a key part of their effectiveness as it allowed unrelated talking and interacting to take place. Invariably mistakes would be made which would make the young people smile or laugh which made them far more responsive to the exercise.

Figure 19: A hero award for going over and above using the language of five keys

As the school grew in numbers we began visiting museums, libraries, theatres, cinemas and made links with filmmakers, poets, writers and a host of creative practitioners. What we insisted on, however, was a clear learning purpose behind everything we did. We wanted to conspire with others to inspire our children and get them hooked back in to learning. The extent of this challenge really hit home one day after a class of Year 5 pupils returned from a visit to the theatre tied in to their topic for that term. One of the boys emerged from the mini-bus beaming and I asked him how the experience had been. 'Brilliant', he exclaimed, before looking a bit distant and confused. 'What is it?' I asked. Unsure, he continued to collect his thoughts for a few minutes before asking, 'Were those people real?'

Now this might seem a simple question but I genuinely struggled to explain that yes, they were real, but they were pretending to be someone else. He seemed happy enough with this and must have thought it a reasonable answer because he went in for his lunch, but it did make us reflect on the magnitude of the job that faced us.

An outstanding in all areas Ofsted inspection followed in our first full inspection with the report stating: 'The curriculum is outstanding. It provides a very wide range of exciting learning opportunities. There is clear progression through developing basic skills in literacy, numeracy and ICT, in addition to providing excellent opportunities for students to develop their personal and social skills'.

Within a few years my leadership role evolved to include leading three SEMH schools on three separate sites, one primary and two secondary.

I was briefed with rolling the curriculum model across all schools and extending the reflective therapeutic approach, but largely I continued to rely on intuition and gut feeling rather than hard and fast evidence. Given the geography of the sites, I realised that we needed help for this to work and approached the educational psychology department of our local authority about creating their first ever service level agreement to help support our work directly. Following a robust interview process, we selected the two most appropriate candidates who had expressed an interest in working with us and made a commitment to producing on-going research as one of our essential criteria. They worked a total of three days per week across all sites and brought a complimentary set of skills that enhanced the support we could give to pupils and staff, thus building capacity.

One of the first exercises we undertook was a PATH (Planning Alternative Tomorrows with Hope) visioning day where we got senior leaders from all three sites together for a day so we could agree and articulate what it was we were trying to achieve together. This helped give everyone clarity around their role and the direction of travel the schools would be undertaking.

I became increasingly concerned that the lack of life experiences was limiting pupil opportunities so we further enhanced our offer by creating the position of a cultural curator to promote the use of heritage and culture to inspire learning. The former head of education from our local museum was duly appointed to post fresh from recently helping the museum win family museum of the year. He was looking for a new challenge and quickly set about forming collaborations with nearly every organisation in the region that was happy to partner with us. Partnership was very important because for collaborations to be successful there needs to be something in it for both parties. A symbiotic approach helped ensure that relationships were sustained for the long term, so a large part of the role was training staff in cultural organisations on how to work with SEND pupils effectively, which ensured our visits were beneficial but also gave something back. We had a wonderfully eclectic mixture of learning opportunities as a result from creating animations with local filmmakers and museum, to boys dance projects, undertaking a pupil takeover of the local motor museum and helping another design their new exhibitions. We made a training video for English heritage staff and got awarded cultural hub status by Arts Connect. I even ended up addressing the National Museum Association annual conference and organising a free conference at The Shakespeare Birthplace Trust to bring educationalists and cultural professionals together.

We also realised that to function efficiently we needed a clear strategy for IT and HR, so we appointed a director of IT and brought in an independent consultant who helped tighten up our policies and procedures, removing wriggle room and reducing ambiguity.

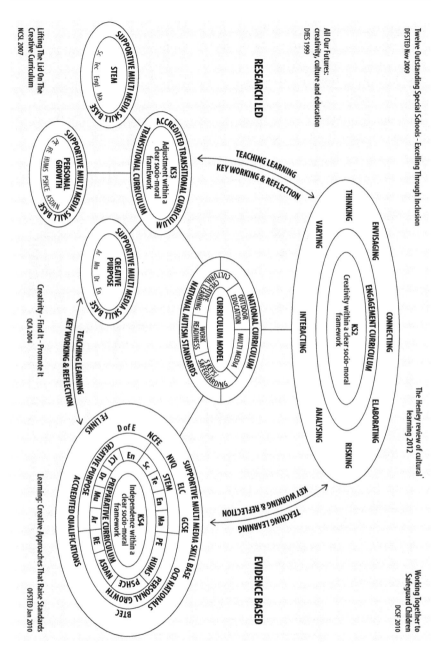

Figure 20: Curriculum model

The curriculum model (figure 20) for Key Stage 2, 3 and 4 schools with a common core of cultural creative learning, multimedia media, five keys/ safeguarding, work readiness and outdoor education. The critical glue that held it all together was the use of key workers in pastoral roles and self-reflection.

The educational psychologists undertook a thorough review of the school as part of their multi-perspectives dimensions framework.

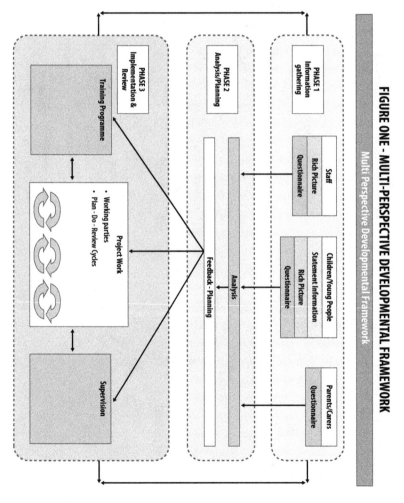

Figure 21: Multi-perspective developmental framework, Harvey , J. and Bartle, D.

It began by eliciting the views of all parents, pupils and staff in the form of questionnaires and rich picture exercises for both pupils and staff. This allowed information to be analysed and the results to feed into a series of working party groups taking responsibility for one of the areas identified as needing improvement. Alongside that was a programme of staff continuing professional development (CPD) and a series of group supervision sessions to support reflection and build capacity.

Themes	Strengths	Areas for development
Teaching and learning	• Students view of themselves as learners • Students as active learners • Cultural and creative curriculum • ICT	• Parents/carers knowing how to support • Role of SM • Homework • Student autonomy • Curriculum delivery • Life skills
Leadership and management	• Nurturing ethos • Child centred approach • Vision of whole school	• Developing whole school approach • Consulting parents/carers about change • Utilising staff expertise • Ensuring staff safety • Student responsibilities
Environment	• Off site activities • Small classes • Comfortable setting • Catering	• Decoration • Comfort/relaxing setting • Outdoor space
Equality and diversity	• Cultural curriculum • Parents/carers feel their views valued • Staff minimising discrimination • Students value diversity	• Cultural curriculum
Communication	• Information shared with new parents/carers • Progress shared with parents/carers	• Whole school collaboration • Joint planning/teaching/review
SEBD	• Discipline based on mutual respect • Whole school vision • Students feel valued • Positive staff attitudes • Key working	• Consistent approach • Use of exclusions • Student ownership of rules
Training Needs	• SEBD • GLD	• Speech and language needs • Attachment disorder

Figure 22: A summary of findings

Rich pictures are designed as an information-gathering tool about complex situations where when pictures are used instead of words, in this case to help capture school strengths and weaknesses. In some instances, pictures can capture themes that may not emerge through just the use of word. The pictures are then analysed by educational psychologists (EPs) to identify common themes.

The working parties functioned across schools, with the support of the EP service to improve their designated areas and the work continued over the whole academic year. The impact varied according to the make up and experience of each group and depending on which staff left the organisation, but they exposed some powerful lines of enquiry that we revisited in more detail in the future.

Through training with the EP service we developed a deeper understanding of additional needs such as attachment disorder. For example we learnt that between 60% and 95% of children and young people with recognised SEMH issues also have communication problems that may go unrecognised (Cross, 2011).[1]

We also learnt about the work of Dan Hughes and his PACE model for supporting a child's self-awareness, emotional intelligence and resilience. PACE stands for playfulness, acceptance, curiosity and empathy, these are all characteristics that adults have to bear in mind when attempting to support young people making sense of their own emotions and be able to self regulate.

Attachment theory

Attachment theory tells us early interaction with a significant person is key. The impetus to communicate may be innate but children will not learn to interact verbally if no one is able to interact with them responsively. If this does not happen early much of their subsequent development is at risk. Difficulties in language comprehension seem to be a high risk factor for the development of psychiatric problems and are an integral part of difficulties such as autism and ADHD.

1. Cross, M. (2011) *Children with Social, Emotional and Behavioural Difficulties and Communication Problems: There is Always a Reason.* London: Jessica Kingsley Publishers.

Adverse environmental factors such as low socio-economic status, child abuse and learning difficulties can all contribute to language and emotional development. Children with undetected communication problems are at risk of being misunderstood, and their inappropriate responses seen as a lack of compliance rather than a lack of understanding that often causes conflict in a mainstream environment.

When severe communication problems and learning difficulties persist after they start school children are at a greater risk of psychiatric difficulties as adolescents (Snowling *et al*, 2006).[2]

The link between attachment theory and communication needs

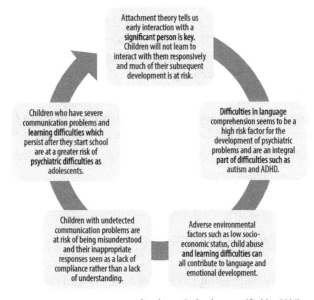

Attachment theory tells us early interaction with a significant person is key. Children will not learn to interact with them responsively and much of their subsequent development is at risk.

Difficulties in language comprehension seems to be a high risk factor for the development of psychiatric problems and are an integral part of difficulties such as autism and ADHD.

Adverse environmental factors such as low socio-economic status, child abuse and learning difficulties can all contribute to language and emotional development.

Children with undetected communication problems are at risk of being misunderstood and their inappropriate responses seen as a lack of compliance rather than a lack of understanding.

Children who have severe communication problems and learning difficulties which persist after they start school are at a greater risk of psychiatric difficulties as adolescents.

Attachment in the classroom (Geddes, 2006)

Figure 23: The link between attachment theory and communication needs[3]

2. Snowling, M. J., Bishop, D. V., Stothard, S. E., Chipchase, B. and Kaplan, C. (2006) 'Psychosocial outcomes at 15 years of children with a preschool history of speech-language impairment', *Journal of Child Psychology and Psychiatry* 47 (8) pp. 759-765.
3. Geddes, H. (2006) *Attachment in the Classroom*. London: Worth Publishing.

In addition to the communication needs of young people being affected by attachment, we helped staff to understand that a child with attachment difficulties may:[4]

- leave you feeling deskilled and worthless.
- really 'push' your buttons, find your vulnerabilities and leave you feeling confused.
- push you to your emotional limits.
- attempt to take control by shocking or frightening you.
- get you to act out of character by shouting or screaming at them.
- make you think they don't need help.
- reject you overtly or by implying they have no need of help.

They often become hyper vigilant, that is they were continually on high alert expecting to detect a threat at any time and respond in a way that will ensure their survival. This state of heightened arousal means they are often ill prepared for learning so we need to create the conditions that would support them to achieve.

Finding ways to help our young people that were rooted in the evidence of what work helped build capacity in our team, who learnt that in order to help we needed:

- firm boundaries and consistency.
- use of additional attachment figure, the key adult to hold them in mind.
- to engage the child's interest.
- to simplify the task.
- avoid failure by helping to remove barriers and solve problems.
- model enthusiasm when success is forthcoming.[5]

As a result of what we learnt through the EP service we began to consider the role of speech, language and communication needs in behavioural issues and duly entered into a service level agreement with the NHS to provide speech and language therapy (SALT). As a consequence of this

---

4. Bomber, L. (2007) *Inside I'm Hurting*. New York, NY: Worth Publishing.
5. Ibid.

multi-disciplinary approach we began to understand more about why we needed structured transitions, clear communication systems, why anxiety/ stress was so important and the need for environmental modifications.

At a time when the Ofsted framework became increasingly defined solely by academic outcomes, many SEMH schools were finding themselves being downgraded by the inspectorate but our evidence based therapeutic approach ensured we were clear about not just what we were doing but why. Our next inspection across all three sites resulted in a good with outstanding features judgment but we were more pleased with the fact that we continued to have no pupils who were not in employment, education or training (NEET) when they left in Year 11.

Realising the operational and strategic risks to having three completely separate schools operating under one Department for Education (DfE) registration, we registered each school separately, which meant greater accountability for each headteacher as they now had responsibility for their own Ofsted report, central register, finances, and so on, and removed the risk of one school misfiring and affecting the Ofsted rating of the others.

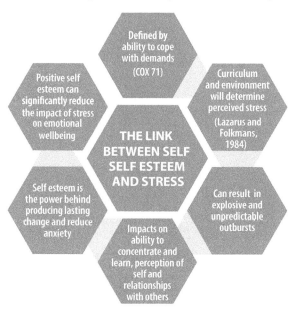

Figure 24: The link between self-esteem and stress

Our diaries and whole school approaches evolved rapidly to make better use of our heightened understanding of needs and creating even greater structure that helped contain anxiety. We stripped things back and made all communication simpler. Staff were trained in visual communication, greater emphasis was placed on environmental modifications and simpler, more child-friendly versions of our keys were produced to increase accessibility for those who struggled to make sense of them.

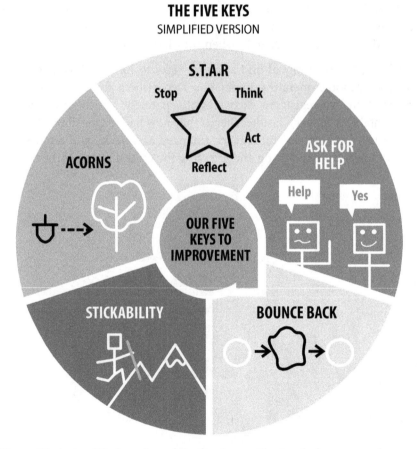

Figure 25: A simplified version of the five keys with visuals for younger learners following input from SALT

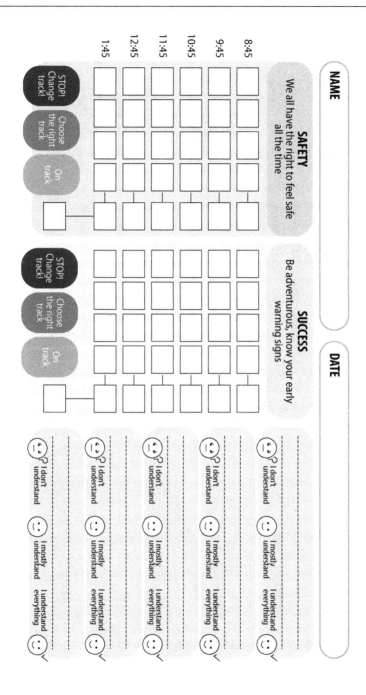

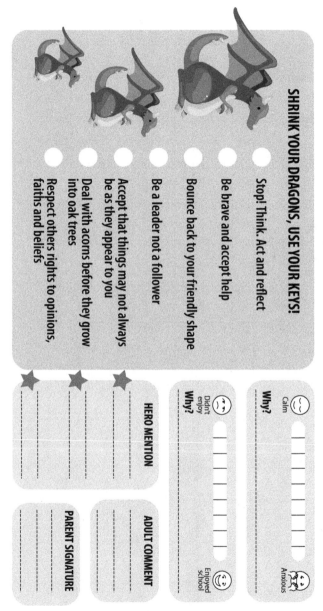

Figures 26 and 27: Single day page from reflective journals remodelled following SALT input

SUCCESS

Be adventurous, know your early warning signs

Arc School Hero

- Challenging yourself
- Accepting a challenge
- Offering help to others
- Going the extra mile
- Meeting targets

On track

- Finishing your work in class when asked
- Accepting help
- Being patient while waiting for help
- Good listening for lesson objective
- Returning to class safely and calmly with an adult

Choose the right track

- Finishing work safely
- Using directed timeout and completing work
- Following steps back to class

STOP! Change track!

- Not finishing work
- Unable to accept help
- Unsafe use of timeout

Figure 28: Clear exemplification of behaviour expectations included in reflective journals following remodelling by SALT

Other modifications included the front of classrooms being cleared of displays and all visual distractions such as open bookcases so that children could focus on the whiteboard or on teacher instruction. An analogue and digital clock, visual timetable and the date were all that were left, as seen in Figure 29 on the following page.

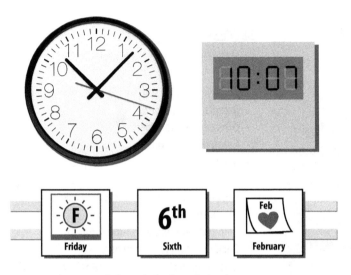

Figure 29: An analogue and digital clock and the date

As we grew we started receiving ever more complex referrals with significantly more specialist needs. We had a number in quick succession of younger children whose behaviour escalated due to acute anxiety, often manifesting itself in extreme behaviours in the blink of an eye. Despite close observation and detailed scrutiny of behaviour patterns there was absolutely no discernible triggers. Thankfully this corresponded with us extending our therapeutic team to include occupational therapists (OTs).

After some joint auditing by with the OTs and SALTs and working under the supervision of the EPs a series of training programmes were delivered focusing on – amongst other things – sensory processing needs and executive function impairment.

Sensory processing disorder is commonly associated with autistic spectrum conditions but once we understood it we began to see it in children within a range of different needs, including attachment and ADHD as well. We began to initiate bespoke therapy sessions delivered by staff under the supervision of our clinicians who were deployed to work at a systems rather than case level. This was crucial because we needed to build the capacity in each school so we had to train staff as one day of a therapists time per school was nowhere near sufficient to meet demand at case level.

The sensory processing assessments were fascinating. They can only be undertaken by a qualified OT and we rarely got referrals with anything specific on other than a vague reference to sensory needs.

Sensory processing disorder is the inability to process sensory stimuli efficiently, for example smells, tastes, noises, touch and so on can be over-sensitive (hypersensitive) or under-sensitive (hyposensitive). The distress caused by over-stimulation can increase the heart rate and cause a fight, flight or flock reaction. Diagnoses with known high incidence of sensory processing difficulties are ASC, ADHD and attachment disorders.

In human beings, all successful learning experiences come from our ability to process and make sense of the information gained from our senses.

We came to understand that sensory processing aided self-regulation, comfort, self-esteem, motor planning, sequencing, motor skill development, attention, impulse control, readiness to learn and the application of learnt materials. It is quite remarkable that given its importance that educationalists understood so little about these areas and it explains why schools don't know what they don't know.

For example we understood about the smell, touch, sound, taste and vision sensory issues faced by children such as the boy who could hear a builder using a staple gun on the roof of a house streets away that sounded deafeningly loud to him or the child who had an involuntary gag reflex to certain smells but we had never heard of the 'hidden' vestibular or proprioceptive senses and how they can be powerhouses of calming for children.

Sensory processing

Proprioception (body awareness)

Proprioception is the sense of body position and equilibrium. Proprioceptors are found in all our muscles, joints, tendons and in the inner ear, they are our muscle sense. They tell the brain whether our body is calm, tense and where it is in space in relation to ourselves and the environment. Proprioceptors play a large role in calming and regulating emotions/arousal levels through deep pressure. Any heavy lifting, pushing or pulling motions or activities crossing the mid-point of the body can help to calm, such as a hug vest, bouldering wall or a stretchy suit.

This is probably best illustrated by footballers before a match jumping up and down in the tunnel while awaiting going on to the pitch and by lots of sports stars chewing on gum. In our context we had a young pupil in one of our schools who was involved in multiple repeated restraints in which he bit staff. The narrative became that he was seeking restraint but we reframed this as being related to proprioception. As a result of a bespoke sensory diet and exercise programme that included the use of a hug vest and a bouldering wall the physical interventions reduced from 29 in one half term to six in the next until they became a thing of the past and the pupil became a successful student ultimately becoming a school council member.

Vestibular sense

This is the first sensory system to develop fully in the womb (by 20 weeks gestation) and it controls our sense of movement and balance. Receptors in the inner ear sense changes in our head position in space and it helps to judge speed, acceleration and direction in relation to gravity to tell us whether we or our surroundings are moving, such as in a train station.

Effective processing of the vestibular system is vital for the development of the stomach and back muscles – the backbone of all motor activity. Children for whom this sense is underdeveloped have poor core strength and often struggle to sit up straight or need to lean on others. This has implications for perception of behaviour in mainstream schools as well as fine motor skills such as writing and cutting out.

Our OT began using the Sensory Processing Measure Main Classroom Form developed by WPS the results of which made for illuminating reading.

The responses are either: 'never', 'occasionally', 'frequently' and 'always'.

Social participation: This student

Works as part of a team; is helpful with others.

Resolves peer conflicts without teacher intervention.

Handles frustration without outbursts or aggressive behaviour.

Willingly plays with peers in a variety of games and activities.

Enters into play with peers without disrupting on-going activity.

Has friends and chooses to be with them when possible.

Uses and understands humour when playing with peers.

Maintains appropriate 'personal space' (doesn't stand too close to others during conversation).

Maintains appropriate eye contact during conversation.

Shifts conversation topics in accordance with peer interests; doesn't stay stuck on one topic.

Vision: This student

Squints, covers eyes or complains about classroom lighting or bright sunlight.

Shows distress at the sight of moving objects.

Becomes distracted by nearby visual stimuli (pictures, items on walls, windows, other children).

During instruction or announcement, student looks around or at peers, rather than looking at person speaking or at blackboard.

Spins or flicks objects in front of eyes.

Stares intensely at people or objects.

Shows distress when lights are dimmed for movies and assemblies.

Heating: This student

Shows distress at loud sounds (slamming door, electric pencil sharpener, PA announcement, fire drill).

Shows distress at the sounds of singing or musical instruments.

Does not respond to voices or new sounds.

Cannot determine location of sounds or voices.

Makes noises, hums, sings or yells during quiet class time.

Speaks too loudly or makes excessive noise during transitions.

Yells, screams or makes unusual noises to self.

Touch: This student

Shows distress when hands or face are dirty (with glue, finger paints, food, dirt and so on).

Does not tolerate dirt on hands or clothing, even briefly.

Shows distress when touching certain textures (classroom materials, utensils, sports equipment and so on).

Is distressed by accidental touch of peers (may lash out or withdraw).

Does not respond to another's touch.

Seeks hot or cold temperatures by touching windows, other surfaces.

Touches classmates inappropriately during class and when standing in line.

Does not clean saliva or food from face.

Taste and smell: This student

Shows distress at the tastes or odours of different foods.

Does not notice strong or unusual odours (glue, paint, markers and so on).

Cannot distinguish between odours; does not prefer good smells to bad smells.

Tries to taste or lick objects or people.

Body awareness (Proprioception): This student

Spills contents when opening containers.

Chews or mouths clothing, pencils, crayons, or classroom materials.

Moves chair roughly (shoves chair under desk or pulls chair with too much force).

Runs, hops or bounces instead of walking.

Stomps or slaps feet on the ground when walking.

Jumps or stomps on stairs.

Slams doors shut or opens doors with excessive force.

Balance and motion (Vestibular): This student

Runs hand along wall when walking.

Wraps legs around chair legs.

Rocks in chair while seated at desk or table.

Fidgets when seated at desk or table.

Falls out of chair when seated at desk or table.

Leans on walls, furniture, or other people for support when standing.

When seated on floor, cannot sit up without support.

Slumps, leans on desk, or holds head up in hands while seated at desk.

Has poor coordination; appears clumsy.

For some children being angry, anxious or under stress means their sensory system is on high alert and we see the senses try to calm the body.

They may:

- become agitated if people get too near.
- not like to be in crowded areas.
- not like changes in environments.
- hurt others.
- seek excessive physical contact.
- have a short attention span.
- be unable to sit and complete work.
- be easily distracted.
- concentrate on one part of a task to the exclusion of others.
- be continually on the move.
- make constant noise.

- hurt themselves.
- rock or jump.

As a result of our training we realised that our structured regime needed more nuance in certain areas. We stopped for example insisting that polo shirts needed to be tucked in, we trialled the wearing of all black trainers instead of shoes and the use of black tracksuit bottoms rather than trousers. What we had noticed was that labels inside clothes often irritated our children. Lots of them subconsciously chose to wear very heavy thick-soled shoes, which helped them to feel grounded but which became potentially dangerous weapons when they were in a highly anxious state. Similarly getting changed out of soft tracksuit bottoms after PE led to lots of heightened anxiety and meltdowns. One frequent offender eventually was able to tell me that the school trousers scratched his skin like wire wool.

What we had been doing had made things worse not better but it was only through the shared learning from health colleagues that we were able to understand why. This is why zero tolerance behaviour narratives are flawed in my view and we will always have to make reasonable adjustments to cater for needs of everyone.

Every time we have worked with mainstream teachers they always notice some of their children in an area of the sensory categories. While teachers are not qualified to make a clinical diagnosis, that can only be done by a qualified OT, they can get a greater understanding of needs. In one of our secondary schools for example it was not uncommon for the students to jump up and hang on to the door frames momentarily while walking down corridors. They would often lead to conflict as the adult perception was that the young people were attention seeking until we understood more about proprioception and looked for other opportunities to give them sensory feedback proactively through structured programmes rather than letting the anxiety build to dangerous levels.

Executive function

In the early stages of life children need safe, predictable and available loving caregivers for healthy development to occur. Their brains develop from the bottom up with the lower parts of the brain responsible for ensuring survival and responding to stress. The upper part of the brain is responsible for a set of skills known as executive function. When stress responses are repeatedly triggered over an extended time period sequential development of the brain can become disturbed and key developmental milestones missed. Children who have experienced multiple traumas quite literally cannot think straight. This doesn't mean they can't learn, it just means they need more support to do it effectively.

Bruce Perry and Bessel Van der Kolk are excellent sources of further information on developmental trauma.

Executive functions consist of several mental skills that help the brain organise and act on information. These skills enable people to plan, organise, remember things, prioritise, pay attention and get started on tasks. They also help people use information and experiences from the past to solve current problems. Having issues with executive functioning makes it difficult to keep track of time, make plans, make sure work is finished on time, multi-task, apply previously learnt information to solve problems, analyse ideas, look for help or more information when it is needed, but it does not have an impact on intelligence.

What are the symptoms? Do you have any children like this?

- Finds it hard to figure out how to get started on a task.
- Can focus on small details or the overall picture, but not both at the same time.
- Has trouble figuring out how much time a task requires.
- Completes tasks either quickly and messily or slowly and incompletely.
- Finds it hard to incorporate feedback into work or an activity.
- Sticks with a plan, even when it's clear that the plan isn't working.
- Has trouble paying attention and is easily distracted/loses train of thought when interrupted.
- Needs to be told the directions many times and has trouble making decisions.
- Has a tough time switching gears from one activity to another (makes change and transitions hard).

- Doesn't always have the words to explain something in detail.
- Needs help processing what something feels/sounds/looks like.
- Isn't able to think about or do more than one thing at a time.
- Remembers information better using cues, abbreviations or acronyms.

Further information and support for Executive Function can be found at the Harvard Centre On The Developing Child www.bit.ly/2zej46e

Once we understood about executive function, everything else fell into place. Suddenly thanks to our evidence based multi-disciplinary approach we understood why structure and routines were so vital and why transitional times and change was so difficult. We had greater understanding why some children were so slow to begin work, why reflection was so key and why we needed to change our whole approach to classroom design and pedagogy. Without this approach we would never have been able to provide as effective support as crucially the support was coming from health professionals and not educationalists. This is a critical flaw in our current system given the lack of any meaningful health input into most schools, even via Education Health and Care Plans.

One key component of this was looking carefully at transitions. We looked at hot spots and flash times where and when incidents occurred and observed transitional times as particularly high risk, especially where they involved movement towards communal times such as break, lunch and assemblies. We virtually eliminated all but essential transitions for some classes especially those new to the school by allowing breaks and lunch to be take in the classroom while we worked on getting them settled and emotionally ready to interact more widely.

An interpretation of school systems in terms of the Maslow hierarchy of needs (Maslow, 1954) and self-determination theory (Deci & Ryan, 2000).

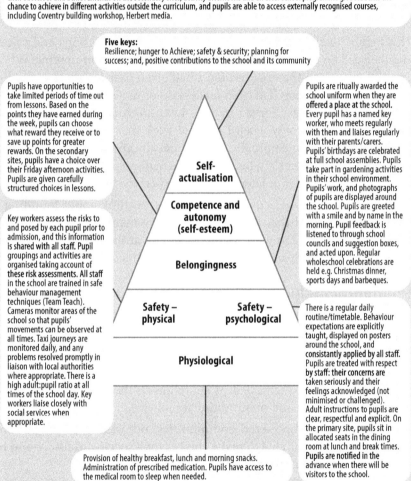

Pupils are taught in small classes, which allows teachers to ensure pupils' work is carefully matched to their interests and skill level. Pupils' work is regularly and frequently assessed, and they are given prompt feedback which draws attention to what they can do. Creative projects and the cultural curriculum give extended opportunities to pupils to achieve and succeed. 'Special mentions' or hero certificates are given out in morning meetings for doing good work or making good decisions each day. Pupils have opportunities to share pieces of their work with the whole school. With their keyworkers, pupils build up a record book of their successes and achievements. On the secondary sites, activity afternoons and an after school programme give students the chance to achieve in different activities outside the curriculum, and pupils are able to access externally recognised courses, including Coventry building workshop, Herbert media.

Five keys:
Resilience; hunger to Achieve; safety & security; planning for success; and, positive contributions to the school and its community

Pupils have opportunities to take limited periods of time out from lessons. Based on the points they have earned during the week, pupils can choose what reward they receive or to save up points for greater rewards. On the secondary sites, pupils have a choice over their Friday afternoon activities. Pupils are given carefully structured choices in lessons.

Key workers assess the risks to and posed by each pupil prior to admission, and this information is shared with all staff. Pupil groupings and activities are organised taking account of these risk assessments. All staff in the school are trained in safe behaviour management techniques (Team Teach). Cameras monitor areas of the school so that pupils' movements can be observed at all times. Taxi journeys are monitored daily, and any problems resolved promptly in liaison with local authorities where appropriate. There is a high adult:pupil ratio at all times of the school day. Key workers liaise closely with social services when appropriate.

Self-actualisation

Competence and autonomy (self-esteem)

Belongingness

Safety – physical **Safety – psychological**

Physiological

Pupils are ritually awarded the school uniform when they are offered a place at the school. Every pupil has a named key worker, who meets regularly with them and liaises regularly with their parents/carers. Pupils' birthdays are celebrated at full school assemblies. Pupils take part in gardening activities in their school environment. Pupils' work, and photographs of pupils are displayed around the school. Pupils are greeted with a smile and by name in the morning. Pupil feedback is listened to through school councils and suggestion boxes, and acted upon. Regular wholeschool celebrations are held e.g. Christmas dinner, sports days and barbeques.

There is a regular daily routine/timetable. Behaviour expectations are explicitly taught, displayed on posters around the school, and consistantly applied by all staff. Pupils are treated with respect by staff: their concerns are taken seriously and their feelings acknowledged (not minimised or challenged). Adult instructions to pupils are clear, respectful and explicit. On the primary site, pupils sit in allocated seats in the dining room at lunch and break times. Pupils are notified in the advance when there will be visitors to the school.

Provision of healthy breakfast, lunch and morning snacks. Administration of prescribed medication. Pupils have access to the medical room to sleep when needed.

Figure 30: A mapping exercise undertaken to demonstrate how we meet the needs of all pupils

As time progressed I was appointed as the National Director of Day Schools for the group, which in reality only added two more schools to my portfolio, but given their distance from each other and the other schools created significant logistical and work-life balance challenges. On numerous occasions I was parachuted in to run one of the schools when they misfired, which they usually did due to making decisions that were financially motivated by the company rather than what was right for the needs of children always taken in pursuit of growth and more profit.

This helped instil a commitment in me to both clear visions and values and the need for ethical leadership to underpin all decision-making. When I parted ways with the organisation I had given over ten years of my life to (and after all schools had been rated good or better at inspection) I was put on gardening leave for six months to ensure that I didn't impact on the business. It was only when I stopped work that I realised how long I had been running on empty for. I was physically and mentally exhausted, I slept like I had never slept before and the realisation dawned on me that had I carried on sooner or later I would have become ill, maybe irrevocably.

Together with a former colleague we began to think about founding a multi-academy trust that could accommodate mainstream, special and resource base provision with moral leadership at the heart of all we did. So the seeds of the framework concept were planted.

Community Education Partnership (CEP) MAT overview

In setting up CEP we were determined to be a values led organisation that built on our collective learning up to that point and did what it said it was going to do rather than what it thought it needed to say. To do that we wanted to be clear about who we were, what we were trying to do and how we were going to achieve it. What follows is the original articulation of our vision, values and organisational model.

Vision: Through empowered communities, our students will become well-rounded citizens able to make choices for a successful future and be a catalyst for social change.

CEP is a community focused multi-academy trust that believes in the holistic development of our children, which will facilitate accelerated learning outcomes for all children regardless of starting points.

We have high aspirations and acknowledge good learning outcomes as essential to the enhancement of future opportunities.

We acknowledge that inequalities exist in local communities however merely acknowledging them is not enough.

We believe that every member of the community has a duty to be an active agent for social change.

We believe CEP can be the catalyst for empowering such change by developing character and working collaboratively with our community partners.

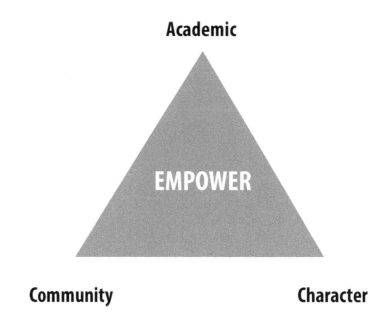

Figure 31: Empower diagram

Community Education Partnership Strategic Objectives

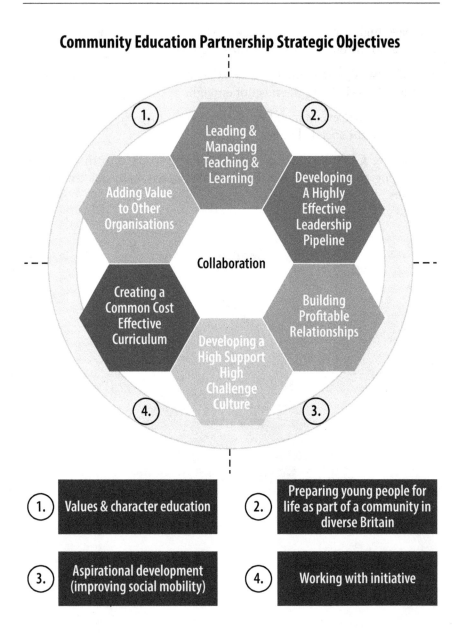

Figure 32: Community Education Partnership (CEP) Strategic Objectives

CEP Values: Academic, character and community

Leading and managing, teaching and learning

We believe in collaboration before competition.

We will work together to learn from each other, celebrating success, diversity and reducing inequalities.

We will collaborate to develop high-quality inclusive provision, meeting the needs of all children.

We will improve outcomes by prioritising professional learning, staff development and creating supportive policies.

Aspirational leadership

We promote transformational leadership to facilitate a pipeline for success at all levels.

Our strong ethos and values encourage all staff to develop professionally.

We celebrate and share genuine outstanding practice.

We acknowledge the creation of a climate where mistakes are views as learning opportunities.

Building profitable relationships

CEP will align with other organisations who share our vision and ethos.

Leadership at all levels recognise the purpose and strength of partnerships to benefit all.

Leaders at all levels will develop opportunities to improve collaborative learning throughout the trust.

CEP will create an ethos where stakeholders look outwards, are informed by research and development to enable our schools to be at the forefront of best practice.

We are committed to a culture of multi-disciplinary working to promote wellbeing and ensure best outcomes for all stakeholders.

High support and challenge culture

We are open, honest and reflective, valuing depth before breadth.

We empower local leaders to lead schools and engage with their local community.

We use research to inform our practice and remain solution focused in difficult times.

We challenge under-performance in schools through focused support and intervention.

We promote pupil voice, equality and self-directed learning.

Creating a relevant cost-effective curriculum

As a trust we share resources and capacity to achieve economies of scale and deliver high achievement outcomes.

Curriculum led financial planning is used to inform our budgeting model.

Each school curriculum is designed to consistently meet the needs of all students regardless of phase, stage of development or educational need.

We put firm emphasis on PSHE as we understand the correlation between the quality of PSHE provision in schools and overall effectiveness.

We acknowledge that social and emotional skills are a more significant determinate of academic attainment than IQ.

Organisational Design

Independent Group Structure which enables close collaboration between schools to lead, shape and develop centres of excellence

SUPPORT
(enablers)
e.g. governance finance, HR, legal, ICT, facilities, etc

DELIVERY
Academic, community impact, services that support the development of well-rounded citizens

DEVELOPMENT
Free schools, research and design, new activities, initiatives

Figure 33: Organisational design

This model will enable different schools to collaborate in shared learning and inclusive school improvement.

Trust model

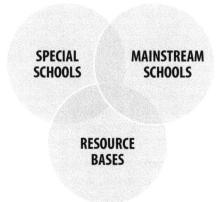

SPECIAL SCHOOLS

MAINSTREAM SCHOOLS

RESOURCE BASES

Figure 34: Trust model

The Community Education Partnership Trust will be focused on Mainstream and Special Provision including Free Schools. This model allows the trust to support the needs of all pupils by providing a mechanism for additional support when needed. It also facilitates reintegration pathways for children to access a curriculum that is appropriate to their needs at a particular moment in time.

Schools will develop working relationships that share best practice in their field to support individual learning needs across the trust.

We spent a considerable amount of time trying to engage with our local authority and the NHS to look at a reintegration model for pupils with SEND variously through a free school bid, an ambitious project to collocate inpatient SEMH provision with an integrated day school linked to local resource bases. This would allow a more nuanced pathway of care both in terms of stepping up but also stepping down back into the community with a focus of minimising inpatient stays, however a combination of the monolithic scale of the NHS, lack of strategic leadership and instability at local authority level conspired to ensure none of the projects reached completion. They did, however, give us lots of food for thought that re-emerged in the Emotional Wellbeing School Improvement Framework and engendered conversations and partnerships that endured.

At about the same time as we were developing the trust concept, I attended the launch of the 'What works in promoting social and emotional wellbeing and responding to mental health problems in schools' advice document produced by Professor Katherine Wear for the National Children's Bureau.

This was a meta-study of international research on what worked in helping promote the emotional wellbeing of students and staff while optimising learning. It focused on six key areas: professional learning and staff development; adopting whole-school thinking; developing robust policies to underpin a supportive environment; implement targeted programmes and interventions; implement targeted responses and identify specialist pathways; and, connect appropriately with approaches to behaviour management.

WHAT WORKS - FRAMEWORK OF EFFECTIVE APPROACHES

There is clear evidence from well-conducted systematic reviews to support schools in employing the following approaches to improve outcomes:

ENGAGE THE WHOLE COMMUNITY

- Engage pupils through encouraging pupil voice, authentic involvement in learning, decision-making, and peer-led approaches
- Engage parents/carers and families in genuine participation, particularly those of pupils in difficulties whose families may feel blamed and stigmatised

Adopt whole-school thinking
- Use a 'whole school approach', which ensures that all parts of the school organisation work coherently together
- Provide a solid base of positive universal work to promote well-being and help prevent problems
- Develop a supportive school and classroom climate and ethos which builds a sense of connectedness, focus and purpose, the acceptance of emotion, respect, warm, relationships and communication and the celebration of difference
- Start early with skills based programmes, preventive work, the identification of difficulties and targeted interventions. Work intensively, coherently, and carry on for the long term
- Promote staff wellbeing, and particularly address staff stress levels

Prioritise professional learning and staff development
- Understand the risk factors to wellbeing, and help pupils develop the resilience to overcome adverse circumstances
- Raise staff awareness about mental health problems and the school's role in intervening early
- Base their response on a sound understanding of child and adolescent development
- Help all pupils cope with predictable changes and transitions, and keep abreast of new challenges posed by technology

Develop supportive policy
- Ensure that there are robust policies and practice in areas such as behaviour, anti-bullying and diversity, including tackling prejudice and stigma around mental health

Implement targeted programmes and interventions (including curriculum)
- Ensure high-quality implementation of specific programmes and interventions
- Explicitly teach social and emotional skills, attitudes and values, using well-trained and enthusiastic teachers and positive, experiential and interactive methods. Integrate this learning into the mainstream processes of school life

Implement targeted responses and identify specialist pathways
- Provide more intense work on social and emotional skill development for pupils in difficulties, including one-to-one and group work
- Use specialist staff to initiate innovative and specialist programmes to ensure they are implemented authentically, then transfer responsibility to mainstream staff whenever possible, to ensure sustainability and integration
- Where pupils experience difficulties, provide clear plans and pathways for help and referral, using a coherent teamwork approach, including in the involvement of outside agencies such as CAMHS

Connect appropriately with approaches to behaviour management
- Respond wisely to 'difficult' behaviour, both responding actively with clear consequences and also understanding its deeper roots, taking opportunities to model and teach positive alternatives

Figure 35: What works – a framework of effective approaches

Professor Weare's findings identify the triggers that can lead to mental health issues such as: a lack of trust; communication and relationship breakdowns; and, the possible lack of extended family ties. The framework builds on this to demonstrate how to engage the whole school community so that pupils feel their voice is heard and parents, carers and families feel they genuinely participate, particularly those of pupils in difficulties who otherwise may feel stigmatized. In order to do this emphasis needs to be put on addressing staff wellbeing and particularly addressing staff life work balance and stress. We need our school workforce to be well enough to care for others to be effective.

She observed that: 'taken together, well-conducted reviews demonstrate that there is a solid group of approaches, programs and interventions which, when well designed and implemented, show repeated and clear evidence of positive impacts on:

- academic learning, motivation, and sense of commitment and connectedness with learning and with schools.
- staff wellbeing, reduced stress, sickness and absence, improved teaching ability and performance.
- pupil wellbeing including happiness, a sense of purpose, connectedness and meaning.
- the development of the social and emotional skills and attitudes that promote learning, success, wellbeing and mental health, in school and throughout life.
- the prevention and reduction of mental health problems, such as depression, anxiety and stress.
- improving school behaviour, including reductions in low-level disruption, incidents, fights, bullying, exclusions and absence.

The evidence clearly demonstrates:

- children with greater wellbeing, lower levels of mental health problems and greater emotional attachment to school achieve higher grade scores, better examination results, better attendance and drop out less often.
- social and emotional skills are a more significant determinant of academic attainment than IQ.

- the strong correlation between the quality of PSHE in a school and the school's overall effectiveness.[6]

The fact that social and emotional skills are a more significant determinant of academic attainment than IQ really struck a chord. It explained why we had lots of bright children referred to the SEMH schools that had steadfastly not fulfilled their potential academically. This is consistent with Daniel Goldman's article Leadership That Gets Results (Harvard Business review, 2000), which says that EQ of leaders is a more important indicator of their effectiveness than IQ. At first glance I was struck by the similarities between what we had already been doing and immediately recognised lots of the component parts.

Prioritising professional learning and staff development

Specialist training from EPs, SALTs, OTs, staff supervision and coaching, de-escalation training, performance management objectives aligned to school improvement objectives, and so on.

Adopting whole-school thinking

School prayer, Five keys, curriculum model, daily staff briefing and debriefing, meeting and greeting at start and end of day, uniform/wellbeing inspection at start of day, undertaking visioning exercise with all senior leaders.

Developing supportive policies and procedures

Calm therapeutic environmental modifications, regularly reviewed and updated policies that reflected changes in procedures.

Implement targeted programmes and interventions

One to one targeted academic support, dedicated individual key workers to provide one to one pastoral support session and link with home and other professionals.

Implement targeted responses and identify specialist pathways

Specialist support where necessary from therapeutic teams, referrals to further specialisms, bespoke learning and behaviour plans, bespoke visual timetables, personalised dietary needs where appropriate.

6. Weare, K. (2015) *What works in promoting social and emotional well-being and responding to mental health problems in schools?* London: National Children's Bureau.

Connect appropriately with approaches to behaviour management

Seeing behaviours as unmet needs, clear reward system linked to reflective journals, personalised behaviour plans, daily score for behaviour linked to safety.

Shortly after Professor Weare's Framework was published Public Health England published 'Promoting children and young people's emotional health and wellbeing'. This outlined an evidence based whole school and college approach drawing on Weare's work and National Institute for Clinical Excellence (NICE) guidance amongst other sources to identify eight principles to promoting a whole school and college approach with Ofsted links to each area.

Figure 36: Eight principles to promote a whole school and college approach to emotional health and wellbeing

It also identified a key question for schools to consider in relation to each of the eight areas:

- How is the school or college providing visible senior leadership for emotional health and wellbeing?
- How does the school or college's culture promote respect and value diversity?
- What focus is given within the curriculum to social and emotional learning and promoting personal resilience, and how is learning assessed?
- How does the school or college ensure all students have the opportunity to express their views and influence decisions?
- How are staff supported in relation to their own health and wellbeing and to be able to support student wellbeing?
- How does the school or college assess the needs of students and the impact of interventions to improve wellbeing?
- How does the school or college work in partnership with parents and carers to promote emotional health and wellbeing?
- How does the school or college ensure timely and effective identification of students who would benefit from targeted support and ensure appropriate referral to support services?

Full report available at www.bit.ly/2Ffh9CU

The links and overlaps with what I had been doing up to that point were clear. It was reassuring that there was a robust evidence base to underpin large parts of what we had done and that our gut feeling wasn't too far off but what if we could have been doing things even better, more quickly and at scale? I realised that I needed to create something that would allow us to build on what the evidence had articulated, but in order to do that we would need to create absolute clarity on what it should look like and how it could be done using a bottom up rather than top down approach.

This prompted lots of reflection and deep thinking as I pondered how to use the learning from our Multi-Disciplinary Perspectives approach to reverse engineer the Framework of Effective Approaches to provide a coherent approach to school improvement. I continued researching what this might look like and produced an initial first draft that would probably have stayed in draft form had one of our acting heads not asked if we had a framework that could inform their work. This accelerated the process and meant that we rolled out the first draft sooner than might have been the case. The impact was stark, it gave senior leaders a rallying point and a clear direction of travel while letting staff know they were valued and other stakeholders that their views mattered.

Through time, as academisation stalled in our local authority an opportunity came along for CEP to merge with a larger nearby trust Washwood Heath MAT, an arrangement which became operational from September 2018. This gave greater financial stability to the new enlarged organisation while giving enhanced leadership capacity and expertise. It also gave us scope to roll out the School Improvement Framework across a greater number of schools, initially through the primary schools but also to secondary, as it evolved into what you will see in this book.

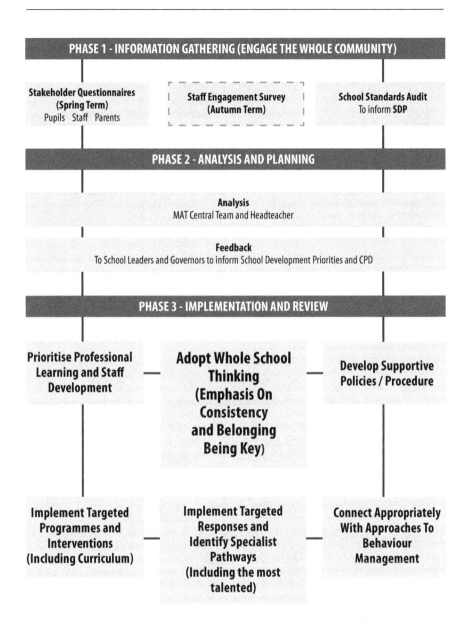

Figure 37: The Emotional Wellbeing School Improvement framework overview

PHASE 3 - IMPLEMENTATION AND REVIEW

Prioritise Professional Learning and Staff Development

- Audit staff skill sets and ensure high quality evidence based CPD that addresses the needs of all stakeholders.
- Encourage staff at all levels to be professionally curious and engage in dialogue around relevant effective practice.
- Maintain accurate staff training registers ensuring training fits school development needs.
- Create bespoke improvement plans to build on supporting staff to improve in a high challenge low threat environment.
- Urgently address underperformance. Prioritise staff not sharing the vision/values or with poor relations with pupils and other stakeholders.
- Understand risk and protective factors in relation to well being and prompt a resilience including mental health and attachment needs. Consider Mental Health First Aid Training.
- Help staff understand and pupils cope with transition and change including within the daily routine of school in order to make it predictable, remove uncertainty and reduce anxiety e.g. movement between lessons, breaks, lunch, start and end of day.
- Build staff understanding of child development, including neurological differences, incorporate environmental modifications and ensure sytems successfully meet needs.
- Create a short, medium and long term career plans for all staff and build in to professional growth cycle. Link to Teachers Standards and SSN code of practice.
- Create tailored CPD for teaching and support staff to harness discretionary effort and empower appropriate individual career progression in line with school development plans.
- Keep abreast of new challenges and opportunities posed by technology.
- Develop robust induction programmes for all new staff including SSN protocols, behaviour systems, assessment and marking, vision and values, non negotiables etc. Link to staff handbook.
- Use staff libraries of relevant CPD materials to inform the evidence base of what works.

Adopt Whole School Thinking (emphasis on consistency and belonging being key)

- Use whole school approaches to create alignment based on clear vision, values and non-negotiables to foster consistant structures and routines that support teaching and learning, remove unnecessary distractions and link financial planning to school improvement.
- Promote a relentless focus on high aspirations and improving teaching and learning through a knowledge based curriculum that meets the needs of all pupils.
- Ensure all staff understand their individual and collective responsibility for improving outcomes in an outward looking, solution focused safeguarding centred culture.
- Leaders at all levels should model empathy and resilience, demonstrating emotional intelligence and positivity especially in the most challenging circumstances. Work should have a sense of urgency and purpose.
- Create clearly defined staffing structures with precisely defined roles and responsibilities. Align them to effective job descriptions that support delivery of the school improvement plan.
- Ensure accuracy of judgements through moderation, triangulation and benchmaking and use it as a coaching opportunity to drive improvements.
- Take time to fully embed new initiatives and avoid initiative overload.
- Promote wellbeing to help prevent problems and improve self esteem by creating time for reflection to promote positive attitudes.
- Emphasise the acceptance of emotion, respect, warm relationships and celebrate difference.
- Research evidence base of what works effectively to improve outcomes, visit other settings. See; The Education Endowment Foundation, What works Centre for Wellbeing, John Hattie Visual Learning etc.
- Promote staff wellbeing and particularly address staff stress levels including a healthy work life balance and boundaried working practices.
- Engage pro-actively with families to forge positive relationships a sense of belonging and work in the best interests of children.

Develop Supportive Policies/Procedures (promoting consistency)

- Ensure that there are robust inclusive policies and practices in areas such as teaching and learning, safeguarding, behaviour and bullying, e-safety and diversity, including tackling prejudice and stigma around mental health.
- Use strong local governance to draw on community strengths to provide challenge and support.
- Use governor portal to facilitate transparent and effective governance, track progress between meetings and engender ongoing professional dialogue.
- Ensure leaders at all levels are free to concentrate on teaching and learning and be both givers and receivers of support.
- Ensure staff handbook includes staffing structure, policies and procedures including teaching learning and assessment protocols to promote consistency. Review regularly to capture new initiatives and link to staff induction.
- Further free up staff to concentrate on teaching and learning by devolving responsibility for fetes, discos, fundraising etc to the local community supported by one named member of staff.
- Ensure new initiative have the time and space to embed through a relentless focus on the objective and doing less of something else.

Implement Targeted Programmes and Intervention (including curriculum)

· Ensure high quality implementation of specific learning programmes and interventions to address reduced progress that are proven to work.
· Be clear on intended outcomes and carefully monitor the impact of interventions.
· Keep it simple and change what doesn't work.
· Explicitly teach social and emotional skills attitudes and values. Integrate this learning into the mainstream processes of school life. See PSHE Association www.psheassociation.org.uk/ , PATHS, Mental security and so on.
· Ensure pupil interventions take account of non-academic needs e.g. risk and protective factors for mental health difficulties, physical activities, sleep, diet, sense of belonging strong adult relationships etc that lay the foundations for academic achievement.

Implement Targeted Responses and Identify Specialist Pathways (including therapeutic)

· Provide more intense work on social and emotional skill development for pupils in difficulties including one to one and group work.
· Use specialist staff to initiate, innovative and deliver bespoke porgrammes to ensure they are implemented authentically then transfer responsibility to staff whenever possible to ensure sustainability and integration e.g. SALT, OT, EP etc.
· Ensure reasonable adjustments suggested above are known, understood and implemented faithfully by all staff through training and effective dissemination.
· Where pupils experience difficulties, provide clear pathways for help and referral, using a choerent teamwork approach, including the involvement of outside agencies such as the NHS.
· Additional support for transitions are routinely accessed by those who need it e.g. visual timetables, timers, personalised start and end of day routines, bespoke induction digital and analogue clocks in classrooms, etc.
· Offer parent/carer support/courses in conjunction with social care/third sector organisations.

Connect Appropriately With Approaches To Behaviour Management

· Look upon 'difficult'/changed behaviour, reduced rate of academic progress or poor attendance/punctuality as a potential manifestation of unmet need/safeguarding issue.
· Respond actively with clear rewards and consequences for behaviour avoiding shame, by offering a facesaving way out through restorative practice.
· Understand the deeper roots of lack of engagement, taking opportunities to model and teach positive alternatives.
· Closely monitor behaviour incidents including who, what, where, when and why and use data generated to spot patterns and build support plans.
· Use of consistent, calm adult behaviour by all staff
· Staff give first attention to best conduct e.g. they focus on praising pupils making the right choices before dealing with those making the wrong choices.
· Relentless, effective routines followed by staff and pupils.
· Scripted interventions used appropriately by all staff.
· Restorative follow up used by all staff to address behaviour incidents and improve relationships.
· Meet and greet successfully used by all staff to aid transitional times.
· Movements around school are ordered, calm and well managed especially at busy times. Pupils walk on the left and show courtesy to others.

Figure 38: The framework

The framework is designed to tell senior leaders what they need to focus on in order to create a high achievement culture with wellbeing at its heart. It supports the 'national standards for headteachers' (which are not well reflected in the Ofsted framework) and is predicated on eliciting the views of parents and pupils via general questionnaires. The staff questionnaire is more specific breaking down each of the six areas into detailed component parts, each one of which is rated on a five-point scale.

This is an attempt to gauge the culture of each school as each individual part can be ranked in order of effectiveness with the lowest scoring areas forming the basis for what needs to be looked at most urgently. Some are quick wins and can be easily rectified however others will take longer and much more detailed planning. In this way, the local community is actively involved in school improvement and their views can help senior leaders decide which areas need to be prioritised first.

To accommodate the schedules of secondary schools we now conduct our surveys in the spring term with a view to planning for implementation from the following September. For our school standards audit we use a current lead inspector and the Ofsted framework to look carefully at performance using it as an opportunity for CPD of staff in how to manage the inspection process.

There has been lots of talk about 'Mocksteds' being a waste of money, unduly stressful for staff and adding to workload, but given the high stakes it's well worth it if used properly as a developmental tool. I think we are obliged to support staff through this process by preparing them fully for it and failure to do so would be negligent. The fact that we use the opportunity to inform school improvement as part of a wider process gives additional validity to the approach, which is welcome by senior leaders.

Our staff engagement survey is conducted by our HR department and is carried out in the autumn term. It looks at the climate of what it feels like in our schools and give useful data broken down into the following sections; about you, your job, your professional development, your wellbeing, equality and diversity, your line manager, communication, your head of academy, how you feel about your academy and the wider trust.

Once all the data is collated it is analysed to find broad themes in each school (see Appendix 4) but also across the trust to see if there are any similarities or differences. Where schools score strongly in a particular area they can offer support to those who score less well which allows all schools to be both givers and receivers of support. The idea is to create a small number of broad themes that capture the main lines of enquiry in a way that is both simple enough to deliver on and specific enough to make real improvements in schools. Any highlighted strengths can help inform school self-evaluation and data can be tracked over time to show evidence of progress. This can help avoid letting areas that have been focused on previously slipping backwards.

This approach has a number of built in checks and balances. Firstly, it demonstrates the involvement of all stakeholders providing opportunities for you said, we did information sharing which helps create a sense of ownership and belonging. It helps check that the Senior Leadership Team (SLT) view is consistent with other stakeholders and if it is not they understand the difference. When things go wrong or are not as good as we should like it is important to acknowledge the fact and move on in order to build trust, giving oxygen to the views of all stakeholders is fundamental in this process. However, it is not always warmly welcomed by senior leaders, especially those who are insecure or do not welcome scrutiny, which is why care needs to be taken to ensure data is collected anonymously and that all views that are collected are not just favourable ones.

As with all analysis context is key. In a school undergoing significant restructuring, for example, it is highly likely that survey results will not be entirely positive. Additionally there are commonly held views that are based on misconceptions they needed to be treated as reality for those who hold them and need addressing. Without asking though schools will not be aware that they exist and may be deprived of valuable early warning intelligence of when things start to slip which helps them remain focused on their main thing, academic progress without damaging emotional wellbeing.

Care should be taken for coordinating the framework by building responsibility into the appraisal cycle of senior staff to ensure it gets done. Surveys where possible should be completed electronically to minimise admin time though some modifications may need to be made for very young children or those with additional needs. One secondary school had nearly 700 responses when they set surveys as homework and other schools have collected views on parents' evenings where access to technology could be a barrier to completion.

When the framework training was launched and delivered to all senior leadership teams and some of the teaching staff, more effective uptake occurred in the schools where training was given to both senior leaders and staff, however the most effective methodology was when training to whole staff teams was given over a number of twilight sessions with space and time built into each session for discussion and reflection.

Implementation would be ideally suited to completing during a whole school Inset day so that data collection could start immediately and staff could get an opportunity to really understand why each component part was important, thus creating buy-in from the start.

So how does it all fit together?

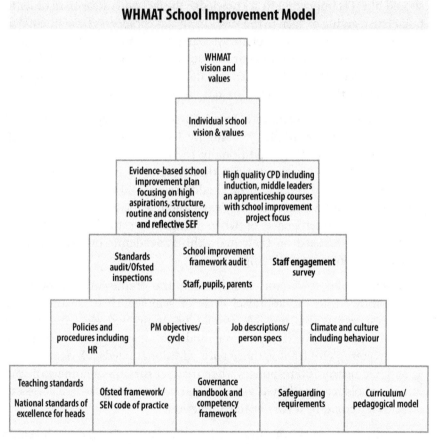

Figure 39: WHMAT school improvement model

This is one view of how the framework sits alongside other processes and procedures in schools. Working out how the disparate pieces slot together to drive improvement can be a useful think piece/discussion exercise to conduct with leaders at all levels.

As part of our desire to adopt whole school and trust wide thinking we began using *Leadership Matters* by Andy Buck as an introduction to leadership for leaders at all levels. It distils the research on how to lead into 40 easily digestible chapters and has a companion reflective journal and a subscription website that contains each chapter in video format as well as a plethora of tools to support leadership development and ensures we have a consistent approach across the trust.

The Leadership Matters model

Figure 40: The Leadership Matters model by Andy Buck

This ensured that everyone had a common understanding of the language of leadership and created trust wide consistency. It helped our senior leaders to stop being as process driven and to do less 'stuff' and more reflective leading. It also put a firm emphasis on knowing your personal dispositions and your context (situation). A subscription to the leadership matters website gave us lots of tools to facilitate leaders gaining insight into themselves and their teams.

A personal disposition assessment is also available free at www.bit.ly/1DiDwe2

The emphasis on climate and culture is reflected in the research behind the new Ofsted framework, which states:

'In drawing together research across these aspects of personal development, it appears that it is not so much individual actions of the school, but attention to climate and culture that matter. School climates that are supportive and nurturing, while also promoting discipline and boundaries, and that actively nurture belonging to school and pupil involvement, show widespread benefits.

Where specific interventions are adopted, it is important to make sure that they fit the context of the school and are implemented thoroughly, consistently and with fidelity.

Interventions most often work if they are implemented in full (Weare & Nind 2011). Evaluations typically show that well-coordinated, whole-school approaches are most likely to have an impact, while uncoordinated small-scale interventions are not. Support from the senior leadership team is essential (Weare 2015; Banerjee *et al* 2014).'[7]

Our situation

Knowing your context is crucial to everyone in education. Pupil tracking data and Inspection Data Summary Reports (IDSRs) give valuable performance overviews and should influence curriculum decisions but other contextual data can help too.

All of our schools are in the most deprived 10% of postcodes in England according to the Index of Multiple Deprivation Data.

Domain	SALTLEY	Tile Cross	W' Heath	B' Mead	Firs	Gossey Lane	T' Cliffe
Income	10	10	10	10	10	20	10
Employment	10	10	10	10	10	20	10
Education skills and training	10	10	20	20	20	20	10
Health deprivation and disability	10	20	20	20	20	10	10
Crime	10	20	10	40	20	20	40

7. Ofsted (2019) *Education inspection framework: overview of research*. London: The Stationery Office.

Domain	SALTLEY	Tile Cross	W' Heath	B' Mead	Firs	Gossey Lane	T' Cliffe
Barriers to housing and services	10	10	10	20	20	20	20
Living environment	10	10	10	40	20	20	40
Income deprivation affecting children	10	10	10	10	10	20	10
Income deprivation affecting older people	10	10	10	20	20	20	20

More information at Indices of Depravation Data 2015: www.bit.ly/1YOhfTh

This mattered because we were concerned about the impact of poverty on our children. We know for example that: 'Up to 50% of children starting school in the most disadvantaged areas will have speech, language and communication needs.'[8] In fact of the first ten pupils screened in Reception in our trust, all had unmet SLCN, including one who needed specialist support from our therapist.

Up to 10% of children in the UK have long-term speech language and communication needs. Knowing the impact of speech and language needs on SEMH meant this could have significant impact on the outcomes for our young people, something acknowledged by The Talking about a Generation report 2017 by The Communication Trust, which recognised that:

- children who experience persistent disadvantage are significantly less likely to develop the language needed for learning than those who never experience disadvantage.
- good language skills are crucial to social mobility.
- it is entirely possible to break the link between language difficulties and disadvantage, with the right support at home, in early education and in school.

More worryingly Ofsted's own data showed that schools in the most deprived areas were much more likely to be rated as inadequate or requires improvement at 21% than those in the most affluent areas at only 5%.

---

8. Gascoigne, M. and Gross, J. (2017) *Talking About a Generation*. London: The Communication Trust.

Most recent overall effectiveness grades of primary, secondary and special schools, by level of deprivation[1], 30 April 2018

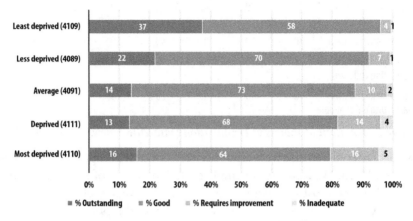

Source: Ofsted inspection data as at 30 April 2018
Source: Schools, pupils and their characteristics: January 2017

1. The indicator of deprivation used in this analysis is 'Eligible for free school meals on any census day in the last six years'.
2. Percentages are rounded and may not add to 100.

Figure 41: Most recent overall effectiveness grades of primary, secondary and special schools, by level of deprivation

To compound this problem further for us The Casey Review: a review into opportunity and integration stated:

'Some minority groups have fared better over time than others. Those (particularly of Pakistani and Bangladeshi ethnicity) with higher levels of residential and school segregation appear to be disadvantaged across a wider range of socio-economic factors. At the same time, some white British communities – particularly in areas of industrial decline – experience significant disadvantage and are increasingly being left behind.

While children from many ethnic minorities are increasingly matching or outperforming white British pupils in education, there is growing evidence of poorer white British boys, in particular, falling behind. White British pupils on free school meals are less than half as likely to achieve five or more good GCSEs as pupils who are not eligible for free school meals.

People from black, Pakistani and Bangladeshi ethnic groups are three times more likely than white British people to be unemployed.

For young black men, aged 16-24, the unemployment rate is 35%, compared with 15% for young white men.

Where they are in work, men of Pakistani and Bangladeshi ethnicity tend to be in low status employment – one in four Pakistani men are employed as taxi-drivers and two in five Bangladeshi men work in restaurants (although a number of these will be in family-owned businesses). Economic inactivity levels remain unusually high among women from Pakistani and Bangladeshi ethnic groups – 57.2% are inactive in the labour market compared with 25.2% of white women and 38.5% of all ethnic minority women.[9]

The population of our schools are largely comprised of such minority groups which means we need to shape our leadership actions and leadership approaches accordingly if we want to create a culture and climate that will build discretionary effort, defined as that which people do over and above what they need to do to keep their jobs, in order to achieve results.

Finally, the risk and protective factors for children and young people's mental health outlined in the Department for Education advice 'mental health and behaviours in schools' – first published in June 2014 and updated regularly since – identifies deprivation as one of the many potential risk factors in the development of mental illness.[10] It is perhaps helpful to first look at what we mean by mental health.

Mental health is defined by the World Health Organization as 'a state of wellbeing in which every individual recognises his or her own potential, can cope with the normal stresses of life, can work productively and fruitfully, and is able to make a contribution to his or her own community.'

The advice advocates creating a whole school culture that goes beyond the teaching in the classroom to pervade all aspects of school life including:

- culture, ethos and environment: the health and wellbeing of pupils and staff is promoted through the 'hidden' or 'informal' curriculum,

9. Casey, L. (2016) *The Casey Review: a review into opportunity and integration.* Ministry of Housing, Communities & Local Government. London: The Stationery Office.
10. Department for Education (2018) *Mental health in behaviour in schools.* London: The Stationery Office.

including leadership practice, the school's policies, values and attitudes, together with the social and physical environment.

- teaching: using the curriculum to develop pupils' knowledge about health and wellbeing.
- partnerships with families and the community: proactive engagement with families, outside agencies, and the wider community to promote consistent support for children's health and wellbeing.

It goes on to details how certain groups are more prone to mental health difficulties due to a range of factors, breaking them down into four main areas: the child, the family, the school and the community. Such risk factors are cumulative and boys under the age of ten with five or more risk factors were 11 times more likely to develop conduct disorder than boys with no risk factors. Girls of a similar age with five or more risk factors were 19 times more likely to develop the disorder than those with none.

It is important that schools know and understand about both the risk and protective factors that can help mitigate the risks, especially for children with less supportive home lives. School has to nurture warm relationships and a sense of belonging to help children feel safe, secure and thrive. Schools should look at how they can strengthen the protective factors especially by targeting non-academic interventions at some groups with particularly high risk factors.

There is much talk of Adverse Childhood Experiences (ACEs), which is when children are subject to traumatic experiences in early life, leaving them more likely to experience executive function impairment.

For more information see Professor Nadine Burkes TED talk How Childhood Trauma Affects Health Across A Lifetime: www.bit.ly/1JlnTKu

This is very important work but we prefer to talk in terms of risk and protective factors due to the ability of schools to redress some of the balance more easily. A report by the World Health Organization in 2004 states:[11]

> There is strong evidence on risk and protective factors and their links to the development of mental disorders (e.g. Coie et al 1993; Ingram & Price 2000). Both risk and protective

11. World Health Organization (2004) *Prevention of Mental Disorders: Effective interventions and policy options.* Geneva: World Health Organization.

factors can be individual, family-related, social, economic and environmental in nature. Mostly it is the cumulative effect of the presence of multiple risk factors, the lack of protective factors and the interplay of risk and protective situations that predisposes individuals to move from a mentally healthy condition to increased vulnerability, then to a mental problem and finally to a full-blown disorder.

	Risk factors	Protective factors
In the child	• Genetic influences • Low IQ and learning disabilities • Specific development delay or neuro-diversity • Communication difficulties • Difficult temperament • Physical illness • Academic failure • Low self-esteem	• Secure attachment experience • Outgoing temperament as an infant • Good communication skills, sociability • Being a planner and having a belief in control • Humour • A positive attitude • Experiences of success and achievement • Faith or spirituality • Capacity to reflect
In the family	• Overt parental conflict including domestic violence • Family breakdown (including where children are taken into care or adopted) • Inconsistent or unclear discipline • Hostile and rejecting relationships • Failure to adapt to a child's changing needs • Physical, sexual, emotional abuse, or neglect • Parental criminality, alcoholism or personality disorder • Death and loss – including loss of friendship	• At least one good parent-child relationship (or one supportive adult) • Affection • Clear, consistent discipline • Support for education • Supportive long term relationship or the absence of severe discord

	Risk factors	Protective factors
In the school	• Bullying including online (cyber) • Discrimination • Breakdown in or lack of positive friendships • Deviant peer influences • Peer pressure • Peer on peer abuse • Poor pupil to teacher/school staff relationships	• Clear policies on behaviour and bullying • Staff behaviour policy (also known as code of conduct) • 'Open door' policy for children to raise problems • A whole-school approach to promoting good mental health • Good pupil to teacher/school staff relationships • Positive classroom management • A sense of belonging • Positive peer influences • Positive friendships • Effective safeguarding and Child Protection policies • An effective early help process • Understand their role in and be part of effective multi-agency working • Appropriate procedures to ensure staff are confident to can raise concerns about policies and processes, and know they will be dealt with fairly and effectively
In the community	• Socio-economic disadvantage • Homelessness • Disaster, accidents, war or other overwhelming events • Discrimination • Exploitation, including by criminal gangs and organised crime groups, trafficking, online abuse, sexual exploitation and the influences of extremism leading to radicalisation • Other significant life events	• Wider supportive network • Good housing • High standard of living • High morale school with positive policies for behaviour, attitudes and anti-bulliying • Opportunities for valued social roles • Range of sport/leisure activities

We know schools need to work to reduce the risk factors while proactively strengthening the protective factors as much as possible. Much of this resonates with what the research tells us about building resilience in vulnerable young people.

- At least one trusted adult, with regular access over time, who lets the pupils they 'hold in mind' know that they care, such as key workers, pastoral staff, head of houses and so on.

- Preparedness and capacity to help with basics, such as food, clothing, transport and even housing. Consider thoughts and emotion sharing box in class and promote their use (not worry boxes!).
- Making sure vulnerable pupils actually access activities, hobbies and sports.
- Safe spaces for pupils who wish to retreat from 'busy' school life.
- Help to map out a sense of future (hope and aspirations).
- Helping pupils to cope – teaching self-soothing or management of feelings through PSHE.
- Support to help others and 'belong', e.g. school teams, class monitors, peer mentoring, school council, lunchtime monitors, playground buddies, reading partners, house systems and so on.
- Opportunities for pupils, staff and parents to understand what resilience is and how they might achieve it.
- Opportunities and capacity for reflection and dispute resolution including scaling exercises to explore feelings and how important an issue will be in the future, for example one month from now.
- Knowing that its OK not to feel OK but that we need to move on.
- Understanding that learning will cause anxiety.

Adapted from Young Minds, Academic Resilience available at www.bit.ly/2IyOJ8E

What everyone needs, and what we attempt to address in our framework is neatly summed up by Viv Grant of Integrity Coaching in this model:[12]

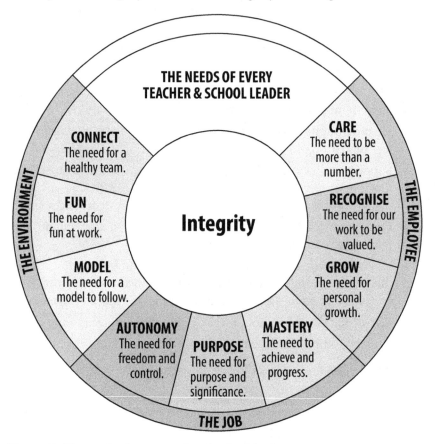

Figure 42: The needs of every teacher & school leader

The restrictive leader

Autonomy and the ability to get good at their job is hugely important in discovering who has the ability to make a difference in schools. Some leaders struggle to let things go and either interfere through micro managing or undermine staff by not giving them the tools to do the job, such as public support or a budget. These leaders serve to restrict the flow

12. More information is available at www.integritycoaching.co.uk

in their systems, like attaching a quarter inch pipe to a one-inch heating system – it will never run at optimal efficiency.

What the framework helps schools achieve is also summed up neatly by Roy Blatchford when he wrote: 'The best schools tighten up to be good but loosen to be outstanding. They recognise the importance of high levels of quality control to secure good provision, evolving into higher levels of quality assurance. Thus a whole school culture of excellence is created within which teachers and students feel empowered to take measured risks.'[1]

Key learning

Remember to consider the impact of stress on increasing anxiety, perception of self as a learner, progress and behaviour.

Be aware of a full range of additional needs including sensory processing, attachment, executive function and other neurological differences.

Know the importance of asking first and creating clarity of vision and values as clarity dissolves resistance and helps rally the herd.

Understanding your own predispositions as well as those around you is necessary to inform leadership choices.

Context is key, know and respond to yours through your leadership choices.

Consider the risk and protective factors and how they can be used proactively to support learners.

---

1. Blatchford, R. (2014) *The Restless School*. Woodbridge: John Catt Educational Ltd.

Chapter 2
Adopting whole school thinking

'Where there is no vision, the people perish'

– Proverbs 29:18 of the Bible, King James Version

(Framework links are bullet pointed)

- **Use whole school approaches to create alignment based on clear vision, values and non-negotiables to foster consistent structures and routines that support teaching and learning, remove unnecessary distractions and link financial planning to school improvement.**

Being able to clearly articulate the vision and values of a school is an essential first piece in the jigsaw of school improvement. Not only do they have to be relevant and useful, they also need to be understood clearly by all stakeholders, as they are the cornerstones that schools are built on. Mary Myatt uses the phrase lived not laminated. Leaders need to ensure that what they aspire to are designed in conjunction with all stakeholders so they are invested and regularly reviewed to ensure that they remain relevant and lived by all. If stakeholders don't know what you stand for, what you want to do, how you are going to do it and why they can't help achieve it.

By painting a vivid picture of a brighter future leaders can invite stakeholders to join them on the journey but they must take into account the context of the school.

One of the many things necessary when supporting schools is to look urgently at how well the back office functions to optimise the amount of money that is available to support teaching and learning. Are procedures robust enough to ensure no financial shocks? Has the budget been allocated appropriately? What are the structures and routines of the school and how effective are they at making schools predictable so children feel safe? All of these questions need to be considered before it is possible to make a judgment on whether unnecessary distractions are allowed to divert from teaching and learning.

Our Core Values

Healthy
We make good choices to take care of our bodies and minds

Aspirational
We believe anything is possible and set goals to achieve our dreams

Resilient
We always do our best and never give up; making mistakes is how we learn

Respectful
We treat everyone with kindness and take pride in our school

Independent
We have confidence to think for ourselves

Figure 1: The HARRI values, the bedrock of practice at Topcliffe Primary

HARRI values form the basis of rewards, assemblies and daily life including running through the curriculum. Like many of our schools it is also a rights respecting school and an inclusion mark flagship school.

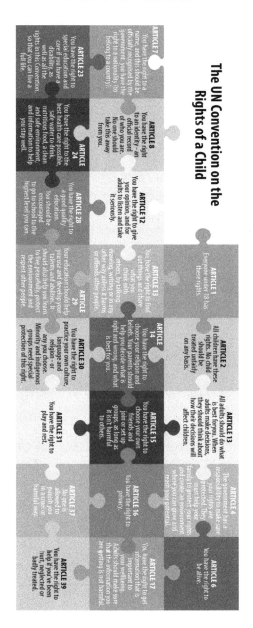

Figure 2: Relevant UN Rights Respecting articles at Topcliffe Primary, which cover the whole wall inside reception. More information at: www.bit.ly/2ic4C8m

Firs 5 Keys to Emotional Wellbeing

Emotional resilience
- Accept that learning will cause anxiety, but still persevere.
- Remember to learn from your mistakes.
- If you can't change something change the way you think about it.
- Believe you can succeed. Say I can't do it... yet!
- Be balanced and flexible and change what doesn't work for you.

Understanding life and its rules
- Understand that rules have consequences that help you make smarter decisions.
- Never be afraid to ask for help.
- Be sensitive to your own needs and consider the needs of others.
- Be a leader not a follower.
- Know that every day is a fresh start. It's never too late to start again.

Planning for success
- Aim high, dream and visualise your success.
- Be honest. Set realistic goals and know what makes you happy.
- Know your best is always good enough.
- Seek solutions, see life as it is but focus on the good bits.
- Create routines that work for you and stick to them.

Respecting difference
- Remember everyone has the right to be listened to.
- Respect the rights of others to hold views different to your own.
- Question to seek the truth in what you see and hear.
- If you hear opinions that worry you, tell an adult.
- Connect with others, listen to their stories and appreciate differences.

Connecting and belonging
- Treat others as you want to be treated. To feel good, do good.
- Make friends with loyal people who want the best for you both.
- Reflect on your day because there's more to life when we stop and notice.
- Aim to be someone people like to be with because of the good example you set.
- Don't compare your insides with other people's outsides.

Routines build habits, habits become character, character becomes lifelong behaviours.

Figure 3: Whole school values approach for Key Stage 2 at Firs Primary

- **Promote a relentless focus on high aspirations and improving teaching and learning through a knowledge-based curriculum that meets the needs of all pupils.**

A relentless focus needs to be put on high aspirations and concentrating on teaching and learning because as David Morrison said, 'the standard you walk by is the standard you accept'. This is the thing that often gets lost when schools are struggling, senior leaders can get caught up doing 'stuff' rather than effectively leading by distributing leadership roles then holding other to account. When this happens it is imperative to slow down, to reflect, to simplify and strip things out so that the wood can be seen from the trees. Unfortunately, failing schools are usually the worst placed to be able to do this and effort can stray from what is perceived to be difficult to things that are enjoyable but don't add value. In short they need to go slower in order to go faster.

We often use the phrase: 'if you are doing something that does not improve teaching and learning – stop doing it!' High frequency, low stake testing should be used to support children to learn and they should be encouraged to self-assess (including homework) to check for understanding and plug gaps. Teachers should aim for a high pupil success rate of 80%, according to Rosenshine 95% is too high as it doesn't stretch sufficiently and 70% is too low as they can be practising errors.[2]

As Stephen Covey put it: 'The main thing is to keep the main thing, the main thing', in other words know your 'it', be able to articulate what it is and make sure it improves outcomes for young people as well as it possibly can.

Class teachers should move away from asking children questions they don't know the answer to and instead tell them what they need to know, then focus on checking for understanding, utilising lots of retrieval practice, knowledge organisers, Cornell note-taking and so on, then starting them from where they are to ensure stretch. It is no longer what I taught them, it is now about what they learnt. Performance can be measured in a lesson but not learning, as learning can only be observed over time and is conditional on what can be recalled and applied in the future.

---

2. Rosenshine, B. 'Principles of Instruction', *American Educator* [Online] Spring 2012. Retrieved from: www.bit.ly/1sOI2mv

This is why inspectors now focus on books over time and pupil progress. It is still, however, possible to observe teachers who do not have good subject knowledge or who do not check for understanding well enough to remove scaffold and support in a timely way to maximise learning opportunities. It will always be possible to detect effective practitioners by observing their classroom practice, discussing pedagogy and observing relationships that foster a sense of belonging. This is a huge change under the 2019 Ofsted framework and will require a change in attitudes from schools, but the sooner knowledge and the transmission of facts is prioritised, the better prepared schools will be for inspection. This is especially true for schools in deprived areas where pupils often lack the experiences that their more affluent peers take for granted. One of the most effective ways to narrow the attainment gap for disadvantaged children is by teaching them facts and using subject specific vocabulary to build schemas and support long-term retention.

'Check for understanding is quite possibly the single most important group of techniques for building relationships with students – I had never fully made that connection before and I suspect many other teachers hadn't either.'

– Teach Like a Champion blog, Doug Lemov[3]

It is important that schools inform children that they will check for understanding to prevent them from failing, but also so that they understand good learning happens far more effectively when learning is tough. That's when we need to draw on our resilience and keep going to reach a successful conclusion. When children understand the 'what' and the 'why' of learning, they are far less likely to opt-out, especially once we remove the fear of failure.

- **Ensure all staff understand their individual and collective responsibility for improving outcomes in an outward looking, solution focused, safeguarding-centred culture.**

3. Lemov, D. (2018) "'It's the most important tool for building relationships", and other insights about check for understanding', *Teach Like a Champion* [Blog] 25 September. Retrieved from: www.bit.ly/2OurG11

All staff need to know that they are professionals and have professional responsibilities that have evolved significantly in the last few years. Leaders need to be clear if schools have evolved in the same way or if there are pockets of practice that have stood still. Some schools look inwards, this is almost always disastrous, as is the fixed mindset that says our children will never be able to do that. Being solution focused is a key attribute for every single staff member no matter who, including cleaners, dinner ladies and office staff as well as those working directly with children. It is especially important that leaders relentlessly model unwarranted optimism as the leader sets the tone for the whole school.

Being outward looking is also important to see what is happening elsewhere and what ideas you could borrow. I have always accepted any invitation to speak about my work as it forces me to take time to reflect deeply on what it is I am doing at any particular moment in time and distil it to its core parts so others can make sense of it. As a result, I have spoken at many conferences and training events but also I have addressed the Women's Institute, parent groups and local meetings of all kinds.

- **Leaders at all levels should model empathy and resilience, demonstrating emotional intelligence and positivity especially in the most challenging circumstances. Work should have a sense of urgency and purpose.**

This is linked to the point above: in times of difficulty everyone looks at the leaders for guidance. They all need a collective understanding of their direction of travel as they will be responsible for the emotional containment not just of pupils but parents and other staff. When driving schools forward, it is important to have both urgency and purpose without overwhelming staff and trying to do too much at once. It's a fine balancing act and one that will not always be called correctly, but lack of action is critical as nothing will be achieved. Knowing your context including the capability of your staff can be a huge help in achieving this successfully by building a high performance culture.

In his book *From Good To Great*, Jim Collins identifies great leaders as being genuinely humble with a reluctance to accept praise when things are going well, rather attributing it to their team or even chance. They are committed to leaving the company in a stronger position when they leave than when they arrived. Conversely, when things are going badly, they do not look to others to blame but first look at themselves. When leaders at all levels adopt this approach schools can really start to develop at pace as it epitomises high challenge low threat.

James Kerr, in his book *Legacy (What The All Blacks Can Teach Us About The Business Of Life)* describes this as leaving the jersey in a better place, so should it be in schools. This is exemplified in a story by John Kirwan, the former New Zealand (All Blacks) rugby player, who when asked what makes New Zealand different explained:

> Last year we'd just lost a game to Australia and in the changing room afterwards I was pretty annoyed. Taking off my shirt, I said something like, 'it's hard to play without the ball' and the captain Andy Dalton tapped me on the shoulder and indicated we should talk outside.

> He took me to a toilet, pointed to a mirror and said, 'John, after a bad game with the All Blacks we look in the mirror and say *could I have done any more for the team today*? And when you've done this, see if you feel like criticising anyone else?' It made a pretty big impact on me.

New Zealand are the most successful international rugby team in the world for a reason.

- **Create clearly defined staffing structures with precisely defined roles and responsibilities. Align them to effective job descriptions that support delivery of the school improvement plan.**

Schools need clarity and staff need guidelines on their specific responsibilities if they are to discharge their duties effectively and be held to account for them. Without an annual review, job descriptions can quickly become outdated and not fit for purpose which can be demotivation for staff and erode discretionary effort. They also need to link with school improvement related to academic outcomes to optimise effectiveness.

- **Ensure accuracy of judgments through moderation, triangulation and benchmarking and use it as a coaching opportunity to drive improvements.**

We are keen to develop staff from within our trust to become leaders through exposure to the School Improvement Framework and a range of other CPD opportunities but that has to start in the classroom. A high challenge low threat culture allows classroom practitioners to be held to account in a way that does not demotivate them or adversely impact on their mental health. External moderation is necessary in order to ensure validity of judgments with the added bonus of being able to share useful hints, tips and resources.

Coaching has many different definitions but broadly speaking it concerns helping others to help themselves by supporting them to learn rather than teaching them. It can help build a positive climate and culture in an organisation when it is done well by ensuring everyone is committed to continuously learning and improving.

- **Take time to fully embed new initiatives and avoid initiative overload.**

Every time we have done surveys for the first time this scores poorly. It is a cardinal sin in schools and is why we advocate going slower in order to go faster. It is imperative that when something new is introduced staff are clear on what they will do less of to make space for it. It is not conceivable in most other industries that new ways of working could be continually introduced without removing something else yet it seems to be a feature of schools.

Change is not something that happens quickly. Humans are creatures of habit. They do not like change so any new initiative needs to be meticulously planned and monitored for it to succeed, just because training has been given on an area does not mean it will happen. In their book *Switch*, Chip and Dan Heath use the analogy of an elephant and the rider. They argue that in order to deliver change you need to:[4]

---

4. Heath, C. and Heath, D. (2011) *Switch: How to change things when change is hard.* London: Random House.

Direct the rider (rational side)

- Find the bright spots – investigate what's already working and clone it.
- Script the critical moves – provide crystal clear guidance with specific behaviours because clarity erodes resistance.
- Point to the destination – know where you're going and why it's worth it.

Motivate the elephant (emotional side)

- Find the feeling – knowing something won't ignite a change, feeling something will.
- Shrink the change – break down the change until it no longer spooks the elephant.
- Grow your people – install the growth mindset and properly prepare for failure.

Shape the path (the situation)

- Tweak the environment – when the situation changes, the behaviour changes.
- Build habits – look for ways to encourage new habits with triggers and checklists.
- Rally the herd – behaviour is contagious, so help it spread.

In schools you also need to prioritise what it is you want to change, be clear on the evidence of why the change is worth making, decide how you will know it has worked, stop doing something else to make room and keep hitting it relentlessly until it sticks. Then allow it to embed. Including all standard operating procedures in your induction programme and staff handbook helps ensure that changes remain embedded.

A useful guide Putting Evidence to Work has been produced by the Education Endowment Fund to help schools' implement research. It talks about treating implementation as a process not an event, one that needs to be planned and executed in stages. In order to be successful the necessary climate for implementation will need to be built with staff understanding the reasons for changes and how it will benefit them and their pupils. This is crucial. Many staff are used to seeing initiatives come and go with little or no impact for the upheaval created. Little wonder that there is scepticism. The Department for Education has been its own worst enemy in this respect over the years, which is what makes a robust evidence base so important. One of the benefits of using the framework year on year is that the direction of travel remains constant so even if senior figures leave the overarching focus of school improvement remains constant thus removing the never-ending cycle of ineffective initiatives.

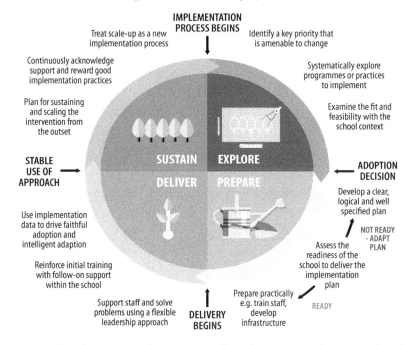

Figure 4: the Education Endowment Fund Implementation diagram taken from A Schools Guide to Implementation, which can be found at www.bit.ly/2OvYh6q

- **Promote wellbeing to help prevent problems and improve self-esteem by creating time for reflection to promote positive attitudes.**

This is something that schools find very difficult to do. We need to be able to find time for reflection and deep thinking. This applies equally to staff and pupils. Schools are very good at getting faster and faster and need to make a conscious effort to slow down or stop. Church schools are often better at this without always realising why what they do helps. Key transitional times in many church schools are marked by a brief pause for prayers at key points of the day, start and end, before and straight after dinner time.

What this does is clearly demark changes, from home to school or from class to break, for example. It also slows the school day down and allows for a brief moment of stillness in an otherwise hectic day. This can be replicated by mindfulness/relaxation sessions, start or end of day reflection or having firm structures that happen in the same way at the same time every day.

Class/form reflection for self esteem, relationships and belonging

These are suggestions for whole-class end of day reflection questions. They can be used as discussion starters if required.

Class ground rules will need to be agreed for reflection but must include that no other pupil names may be used nor anything that identifies others in the school unless it is in a positive light.

Additional questions can be developed with the children. Rewards could be built in to celebrate success. Try to link to school values and other initiatives.

Do you feel you have had the chance to contribute today?

Do you feel you have been listened to today?

Did you find anything tricky today? How did you cope/manage it?

Who has helped you today?

How have you helped others?

Who did you see doing well today?

How did you stay active and healthy today?

What was your proudest achievement today?

What did you enjoy learning most today?

How have you been as a learner today, Give yourself a score out of 10 with 0 being the lowest and 10 being the highest.

What do you need to do to improve this score tomorrow?

What made you feel good today?

Who would you like to nominate for going over and above today and why? (This must not be a close friend!)

The Sumo Guy (Paul McGee) has created Sumo for schools based on his best selling book SUMO (Shut up and Move on). It supports pupil reflection by encouraging them to SUMO (Stop, Understand, Move On). When faced with a challenge children are encouraged to ask themselves:

- Where is this on a scale of 1 to 10?
- How important will this be in six months?
- Is my response appropriate and effective?
- How can I influence or improve the situation?
- What can I learn from this?
- What will I do differently next time?
- What can I find that's positive in this situation?

This can encourage discussion and aid self reflection when practiced over time. More details available at www.sumo4schools.com

Effective leaders read round their subject but they also need to make space for deep thinking around how what they have read is relevant to their context. When I met with senior EPs in the past, we set aside time and tried as much as possible to go walking outside while we thought about what we had to do. We could have sat in a meeting room to do this but the quality of our outcomes were always much better when we had created the conditions for our thoughts to free flow. Turning the radio off on a long commute, exercising in the gym, swimming, walking the dog or cycling can create other opportunities for deep thinking.

Deep thinking cannot happen without creating the time and space for it to flourish by practicing it repeatedly. Capturing thoughts on the move using digital devices can ensure that your thinking can happen anywhere, sometimes when you least expect it because 'the brain hides more from you than it reveals. Therefore the unconscious aspects of your mind are the most of your mind.'[5]

Accepting all opportunities to speak at events helps distil practice to its fundamentals and make sense of where you are in your thinking. Creating conditions for staff to do the same through presenting to governors, parents, across schools or with local networks helps build a reflective learning culture that supports staff development.

Creating the correct culture and climate in the workplace is very important in promoting wellbeing. The World Health Organization (WHO) describe risk factors to mental health in the work place as follows:[6]

Risk factors:

- Inadequate health and safety policies.
- Poor communication and management practices.
- Limited participation in decision-making or low control over one's area of work.
- Low levels of support for employees.
- Inflexible working hours.
- Unclear tasks or organisational objectives.

Risks may also be related to job content, such as unsuitable tasks for the person's competencies or a high and unrelenting workload. Some jobs may carry a higher personal risk than others (e.g. first responders and humanitarian workers), which can have an impact on mental health and be a cause of symptoms of mental disorders, or lead to harmful use of alcohol or psychoactive drugs. Risk may be increased in situations where there is a lack of team cohesion or social support.

It goes on to outline what organisations can do to create health workplaces including:

---

5. O'Brien, T. (2015) *Inner Story: Understand your mind. Change your world.* Scotts Valley, CA: CreateSpace Independent Publishing.
6. World Health Organization (2019) Mental health in the workplace: Information sheet. Retrieved from: www.bit.ly/2DhUgfZ

- Awareness of the workplace environment and how it can be adapted to promote better mental health for different employees.
- Learning from the motivations of organisational leaders and employees who have taken action.
- Not reinventing the wheel by being aware of what other companies who have taken action have done.
- Understanding the opportunities and needs of individual employees, in helping to develop better policies for workplace mental health.
- Awareness of sources of support and where people can find help.

Before describing interventions and good practices that protect and promote mental health in the workplace which include:

- implementation and enforcement of health and safety policies and practices, including identification of distress, harmful use of psychoactive substances and illness and providing resources to manage them.
- informing staff that support is available.
- involving employees in decision-making, conveying a feeling of control and participation – organisational practices that support a healthy work-life balance.
- programmes for career development of employees.
- recognising and rewarding the contribution of employees.

The parallels to education in this are self-evident, can clearly be seen reflected throughout our framework and they should form the basis for discussion amongst leaders at all levels.

- **Emphasise the acceptance of emotion, respect, warm relationships and celebrate difference.**

We know emotional intelligence is a better indicator of academic attainment and good leadership than IQ. Knowing our own pre-dispositions is a key component to engaging with others effectively. Respect, genuine warmth and being able to celebrate differences are key characteristics of being emotionally aware. Working conditions and relationships are both highly important for improving staff retention, however leadership dynamics in schools are the strongest indicator of staff retention where they are based on fairness, respect and staff engagement.[7]

Celebrating difference is particularly important to break down barriers between communities, especially those that are inward looking because without us teaching difference in schools such communities will remain isolated in the future to the detriment of young people and wider society. In one school, a female Year 11 student commented that what she liked about school was that it taught her things her parents wouldn't let her know about.

Schools have a duty to prepare young people for life in modern Britain as outlined in DfE advice on promoting basic important British values as part of pupils' spiritual, moral, social and cultural (SMSC) development which makes it clear that:

'Schools should promote the fundamental British values of democracy, the rule of law, individual liberty, and mutual respect and tolerance of those with different faiths and beliefs. This can help schools to demonstrate how they are meeting the requirements of Section 78 of the Education Act 2002, in their provision of SMSC.[8]

Actively promoting the values means challenging opinions or behaviours in school that are contrary to fundamental British values. Attempts to promote systems that undermine fundamental British values would be completely at odds with schools' duty to provide SMSC. The Teachers' Standards expect teachers to uphold public trust in the profession and maintain high standards of ethics and behaviour, within and outside school. This includes not undermining fundamental British values.'

- **Research evidence base of what works effectively to improve outcomes, visit other settings. See: The Education Endowment Foundation, What Works Centre for Wellbeing and Doug Lemov's work.**

It is only recently that the concept of using evidence to inform practice has taken a hold in education. One reason for that may be the perception that it is difficult to isolate the multiple different factors of school life

---

7. Edurio (2019) 'Improving Staff Retention in Academies'. London: Edurio.
8. Department for Education (2014) 'Promoting fundamental British values through SMSC'. London: The Stationery Office.

to identify what has made the difference to learning. There is also disconnect between complex academic papers and what it looks like in practice, especially for the busy classroom practitioner. Fortunately that is starting to change with organisations beginning to distil research into more school friendly formats.

Examples of this include those mentioned above as well as websites such as The Learning Scientist, Institute for Effective Education, Research Schools Network, The Chartered College of Teaching and ResearchEd. A number of other writers cover this area, many of whom have blogs or you can find on Twitter, including David Didau, Tom Sherrington, Daniel Willingham, Daisy Christodoulou and Stephen Tierney, amongst many.

Teaching and Learning Firs Primary School

Firs Foundations of Effective Teaching Practice

F1 - Checking For Understanding (CFU)

At Firs Primary School we will embed a common language of *'they learnt it'* rather than *'I taught it'* and *'I am learning...'* rather than *'I am doing...'* to prioritise learning. We encourage staff not to assume understanding but confirm it (assure don't assume).

There are also two ways in which staff at Firs will develop CFU at Firs Primary School.

Firstly, *information gathering* - using summative and formative methods of assessment to gather data and inform teaching practice; allowing the teacher to be responsive to the needs of a class, individual child or group of children.

Secondly, effectively using assessment information and developing a culture of learning from our mistakes.

The schools <u>marking and feedback policy</u> fully supports *live marking* in the classroom; picking up on misconceptions and redirecting learning as required.

F3 - Teaching and Learning Ratios; thinking and participation (80:20)

Teachers at Firs are encouraged to ensure children complete as much of the cognitive thinking as they can through; *questioning, writing* and *discussion*. Teaching and Learning ratios will be broken down into two different ways of delivery. Thinking Ratio (*how rigorous is the work?*) and Participation on Ratio (*how many children are actively engaged and participating?*) are two important factors teachers at Firs will seek to master to ensure academic rigour within the classroom.

Children cannot achieve academic rigour unless they learn lots of content knowledge themselves.

Thinking Ratio will refer to the level of engagement, depth and quality of learning taking place in our classrooms. Participation Ratio refers to learners being actively engaged in their learning and not merely passengers in a lesson. Time on task is a driving factor in achieving academic rigour in our classrooms and ensuring children are thinking and participating at a maximal level.

F2 - Academic Ethos

At Firs Primary School we encourage staff to create and deliver lessons to achieve the maximum level of academic rigour. We aim to create an ethos in which children are challenged to *think, perform*, and *grow* to a level that they were not at previously.

This involves teachers setting high expectations, planning for success, creating a lesson structure and ensuring pace (*time on task*) is a key driver.

Staff at Firs Primary School are expected to create environments in which the maximal level of academic rigour is expected, practiced and valued by *all* children.

F4 - A Culture and Climate for Learning

Developing a positive learning culture and climate in the classroom will only improve academic outcomes and achievement at Firs Primary School. There are two main drivers in establishing a positive learning climate and culture at Firs.

Firstly: the main purpose of the classroom is to promote academic learning.

Secondly: the culture and expectations are positive, engaging, joyful, caring and productive.

Discipline - the process of teaching children the right and successful ways to do things. Children at Firs Primary are expected to follow the school charter and be *Ready, Respectful* and *Safe* at all times.

Management - effective classrooms require effective management systems. Teachers at Firs Primary are encouraged to reinforce expectations to further embed positive attitudes to learning.

Control - strong control in the classroom at Firs relates to the *power of affective/effective language* and the ability to *develop strong relationships*. At Firs Primary we prioritise in ensuring children feel that they belong and connect to the classroom and school.

Influence - at Firs Primary we want our children to believe in what they are doing during lessons. The class teacher will be responsible for influencing children to '*believe*' and not just '*behave*' during lessons. *We expect all staff to instill a love of learning in every child*.

Engagement - children's minds will only be engaged during lessons in which teachers allow children to have plenty to do and plenty to get involved in. Teachers at Firs will engage children though important, interesting and challenging work.

Firs Foundations of Effective Practice

Figure 5: Firs Primary School 'Foundations of Teaching and Learning', drawing on the work of Doug Lemov and Teach Like a Champion

Evidence does not necessarily mean articles in peer review journals: it could simply mean what works in similar settings. That could be in another year group or department in a school, it may be a school in similar circumstances or it could mean published reports, professional journals, the Education Endowment Foundation, ResearchEd and so on. Using what is proven to work in similar circumstances can save lots of time and effort by avoiding reinventing the wheel.

Social media can be a very helpful way of keeping up to date with current research and tracking debate in education, especially Twitter. By judiciously following individuals or organisations in a specific area, busy teachers can keep up relatively easily with the latest thinking and debate. All staff should be encouraged to use social media, but they must be made aware of relevant policies in order to do so safely and without putting themselves in a vulnerable position.

In his great book on teaching, Tom Sherrington breaks research down in to three general categories: classroom climate, principles of instruction and memory. He also sites numerous useful research sources that are an invaluable starting point for improving teaching and learning including: Barak Rosenshine's Principles of Instruction; the Education Endowment Fund Toolkit; Dylan Williams' blog entry 'nine things every teacher should know'; The Learning Scientists website; John Hattie's *Visible Learning*; Daniel Willingham's *Why Don't Students Like School?*; Professor Robert Coe's (*et al*, 2014) report 'what makes great teaching?'; David Didau and Nick Rose's *What Every Teacher Needs to Know about Psychology*; and, John Sweller's 'Cognitive Load Theory'. A number of these can be downloaded free online.[9]

A particularly useful starting point is John Tomsett's blog on Cognitive Load Theory.[10] This refers to the limitations on learning when working memory capacity is exceeded by a learning task. Working memory is short term and finite where as long-term memory is infinite so the

9. Sherrington, T. (2017) 'Teaching and Learning Research Summaries: A collection for easy access'. *Teacherhead* [Online] 3 June. Retrieved from: www.bit.ly/2r62gwd
10. LeadingLearner (2019) 'Cognitive Load Theory Updated; 20 Years On – Implications for Teachers and Teaching'. *@LeadingLearner* [Online] 10 February. Retrieved from: www. bit.ly/30VeRiN

movement of knowledge from short to long-term memory in its simplest terms aids learning, especially for disadvantage learners. Dylan Williams tweeted that he had come to the conclusion that John Sweller's Cognitive Load Theory is the single most thing for teachers to know.

Tom Sherrington's blog about Rosenshine's Principles of Instruction leads naturally on from there.[11] Rosenshine presented an article with ten research-based principles of instructions along with recommendations for classroom practice: namely daily review, weekly review, asking questions , checking for understanding, presenting new materials using small steps, provide models, provide scaffold for difficult tasks , guide student practice, obtain a high success rate (80%+) and independent practice. The principles drew upon research in cognitive science, research on master teachers and research on how to give cognitive supports to help students learn complex tasks. Sherrington splits these into four broad areas of reviewing materials, questioning, sequencing concepts and modelling and stages of practice. In short, this represents quality first teaching but understanding the component parts of good teaching helps staff to understand which bits they need to focus on to improve outcomes

Ross Morrison McGill also has a wonderful blog that contains multiple resources to support teaching and learning including the five-minute lesson plan and a useful infographic showing organisations with the greatest influence on shaping policy.[12] The prominence of the education endowment foundation, FFT education datalab and the Sutton trust makes it worth following them closely. Horizon scanning is a key leadership attribute that can easily get overlooked in the busy lives of school leaders, as is reading and reflecting on practice.

Chris Moyse has collected a number of useful research papers and article available on his website.[13]

11. Sherrington, T. (2018) 'The Roots of Rosenshine's Principles'. *Teacherhead* [Online] 14 December. Retrieved from: www.bit.ly/33nb3sn
12. Morrison McGill, R. (2019) *@TeacherToolkit*. Retrieved from: www.bit.ly/2pfNrEL
13. Moyse, C. (2016) 'Research Articles'. *Chris Moyse TLC Education Services Limited* [Online] 28 October. Retrieved from: www.bit.ly/33cjJ4v

- **Promote staff wellbeing and particularly address staff stress levels including a healthy life work balance and boundaried working practices.**

Not to oversimplify this but if staff do not have a healthy life work balance (yes it should be that way around) then they cannot give of their best to caring for our young people. You simply can't put children first if you put teachers last. Staff are on the frontline day after day and schools need to boundary their working especially in the modern age when e mails are often picked up on mobile devices outside work hours. Some senior leaders argue that they like to work in the evenings to keep on top of their to-do list or would rather be contactable so they know what's going on. That is fine in so far as it goes but any organisation takes its lead from the top and so it is imperative that senior leaders model the boundaries (the obvious exception being any safeguarding issues). By all means write emails after an agreed time but leave them in your draft box and send them during agreed working hours. Staff need time away from school both physically and emotionally, not least to make time to do the things that keep them well such as being with family and friends, exercising, getting outside, pursuing hobbies and so on. Unboundaried working risks drawing them back into schools mentally, which detracts from this and, therefore, is counterproductive and harmful.

The Education Support Partnership is a charity providing mental health and wellbeing support to all education staff and organisations and is worth sign posting to all staff.

Useful resources to support mental health can be found on the Mental Health First Aid website.

The Teacher Wellbeing Index 2018 gives a vivid illustration why we can't afford to ignore this sensitive subject. It reports that 67% of teachers are stressed at work, 74% report an inability to switch off and relax to be the main contributor to a negative work/life balance, 29% work more than 51 hours a week on average, 31% experienced a mental health issue in the past year and 72% attribute workload as the main reason for considering leaving their jobs. Despite this 65% say they wouldn't feel confident in disclosing mental health problems or unmanageable stress to their employer and 36% say they have no form of mental health support at work. Further information can be found on the Education Support Partnership website.[14]

If we do not start addressing this seriously the current staffing shortages will be exacerbated further, stretching staff even more, leading to greater staff shortages in an escalating spiral.

- **Engage proactively with families to forge positive relationships, a sense of belonging and work in the best interests of children**

Families are a wonderful resource for better understanding their children. It is easy to label certain pupils or families as troublesome and create barriers and alienation. This will be a powerful disincentive for pupils feeling a sense of belonging. It is, therefore, important to reach out to families on the periphery of our communities when things are going well rather than when things go badly. They often may have had negative experiences with school specifically and authority figures more generally. Positive interactions, genuinely seeking their opinion and letting them know it is valued will stand schools in very good stead when they need support or when things get difficult. It will also make them more receptive to being open and engaging with school, which is why we need to be relentlessly positive about our ability to engage with all parents.

Key learning

Don't make stuff up! Research the evidence base of what works effectively in similar schools and adapt them to suit your context. Constantly scan the horizon to know what might be coming next.

Collect the views of all stakeholders to inform school improvement. Some of it may be painful but it can be a powerful driver for improving culture in schools by empowering others to influence change and bringing them with you on the journey.

Great leaders are inherently humble. When things are going well they look out the window to praise their team, attribute success to external factors or luck. When they are going badly they look in the mirror. They always seek to leave the organisation in a stronger when they leave than when than when they arrived.

14. Education Support Partnership (2018) 'Teacher Wellbeing Index 2018'. Retrieved from: www.bit.ly/2RkJF8a

Meticulously plan new initiatives and treat implementation as a staged process. Remember to direct the rider, motivate the elephant and flatten the path.

Staff should be supported to remain outward looking and solution focused even in the most challenging times by creating a psychologically safe space for staff at all levels to engage in challenge and debate.

Leaders at all levels should be emotionally aware and use their emotional intelligence to influence decision-making. Ensure staff have emotional permission to create time and space for reflection by adopting a whole school approach.

Create a boundaried working culture from the top down that promotes a healthy work life balance and shows staff you care about them because what you permit you promote.

Low challenge high frequency testing and retrieval practice helps support the transfer of knowledge from short to long-term memory, reducing cognitive load and improving learning.

Reflective audit

In answer to 'How well do we do this?', please give a single score to reflect where we are now based on:

1. Lack of consistent awareness among staff.
2. Some emerging awareness.
3. Increasing consistency with evidence of improving outcomes.
4. Embedded practices familiar to all staff and Included in staff handbook and induction programmes. Staff routinely engage in professional dialogue to reflect on pupil learning and challenge orthodox thinking.
5. Strong evidence of embedded practice and improved outcomes. Senior leaders supporting in other settings.

In answer to priority please RAG rate based on:

Red = High priority

Amber = Medium priority

Green = Low priority

Adopt whole school inclusive thinking (Emphasis on consistency being key)	How do you do this?/ What do you do?	How well does the school do this now? 1-5	How much of a priority is it? RAG rate	What actions might the school take?
Use whole school approaches to create alignment based on clear vision, values and non-negotiables to foster consistent structures and routines that support teaching and learning, remove unnecessary distractions and link financial planning to school improvement.				
Promote a relentless focus on high aspirations and improving teaching and learning through a knowledge-based curriculum that meets the needs of all pupils.				
Ensure all staff understand their individual and collective responsibility for improving outcomes in an outward looking, solutions focused, safeguarding centred culture.				
Leaders at all levels should model empathy and resilience, demonstrating emotional intelligence and positivity especially in the most challenging circumstances. Work should have a sense of urgency and purpose.				
Create clearly defined staffing structures with precisely defined roles and responsibilities. Align them to effective job descriptions that support delivery of the school development plan.				

Adopt whole school inclusive thinking (Emphasis on consistency being key)	How do you do this?/ What do you do?	How well does the school do this now? 1-5	How much of a priority is it? RAG rate	What actions might the school take?
Ensure accuracy of judgments through moderation, triangulation and benchmarking and use it as a coaching opportunity to drive improvements.				
Take time to fully embed new initiatives and avoid initiative overload.				
Promote wellbeing to help prevent problems and improve self-esteem by creating time for reflection to promote positive attitudes.				
Emphasise the acceptance of emotion, respect, warm relationships and celebrate difference.				
Research evidence base of what works effectively to improve outcomes, visit other settings. See: The Education Endowment Foundation, What Works Centre for Wellbeing, ResearchEd, Chartered College, Doug Lemov, John Hattie, and so on.				
Promote staff wellbeing and particularly address staff stress levels including a healthy life work balance and boundaried working practices.				
Engage proactively with families to forge positive relationships, a sense of belonging and work in the best interests of children.				

Potential action plan

Main priority areas (Low scoring and high priority)	Action needed	Evidence base	What will you do less of?	Link to Ofsted framework

Chapter 3
Prioritising professional learning and staff development

'When you want to help people, you tell them the truth. When you want to help yourself you tell them what they want to hear.'

– Thomas Sowell

- **Audit staff skill sets and ensure high quality, evidence-based CPD that addresses the needs of all stakeholders.**

Auditing the skills of staff is vitally important to help understand your context. It cannot be assumed that all staff share the same level of experience or training and without knowing what skill sets staff have or what areas they need to have developed in order to deliver effective staff training and personalised CPD.

The DfE standard for teachers' professional development states:

Effective teacher professional development is a partnership between:

- *Headteachers and other members of the leadership team*
- *Teachers*
- *Providers of professional development expertise, training or consultancy*

In order for this partnership to be successful:

1. *professional development should have a focus on improving and evaluating pupil outcomes.*

2. *professional development should be underpinned by robust evidence and expertise.*

3. *professional development should include collaboration and expert challenge.*

4. *professional development programmes should be sustained over time.*

And all this is underpinned by, and requires that:

5. *Professional development must be prioritised by school leadership.*

The standard for teachers' professional development is available to download on the Department for Education website.[1]

- **Encourage staff at all levels to be professionally curious and engage in dialogue around relevant effective practice.**

Discussion in schools around effective practice is something that should be encouraged, be it sharing useful websites, resources or approaches to learning. Unless this is facilitated in some way by senior leaders this is something that can gets lost in busy schools yet it is useful for improving outcomes and reducing workload when done effectively. We use coaching extensively to heat map individual practice linked to Ofsted criteria and work to target very specific teaching techniques as described by Doug Lemov in *Teach like a Champion* to rapidly improve teaching and learning. This creates a psychologically safe space where less than optimum performance can be discussed openly and staff helped to improve. This is a prerequisite of high performing teams and can have a protective effect on mental health.

- **Maintain accurate staff training registers ensuring training fits school development needs.**

As well as auditing staff skills, schools also need to track what training staff are undertaking and plan for it accordingly. This is contingent on knowing the career aspirations of staff in the short, medium and long term, as well as the situation of the school. Training needs to fit the school development plans and build on the existing skills of staff to be effective.

---

1. Department for Education (2016) Standard for teachers' professional development: Implementation guidance for school leaders, teachers, and organisations that offer professional development for teachers. London: The Stationery Office.

For this to happen though staff must also know what they want to achieve in their career and suggest suitable training opportunities for themselves.

- **Create bespoke improvement plans built on supporting staff to improve in a high challenge low threat environment.**

Staff at all levels need to have bespoke plans to improve their performance for a school to truly have a continuous improvement model in place. Chris Moyse talks about professional growth rather than performance management and tweets widely on the approach his trust have adopted, which is based on a compassionate model of working with staff.

Doug Lemov's *Teach Like A Champion* work, emanating from the Charter School Movement in the US, identifies 62 techniques to put students on the path to college and is a very useful starting point to help staff improve. It includes video exemplars of the techniques in practice. Understanding the techniques can help develop consistent staff vocabulary about what makes effective learning and help facilitate pedagogical discussions. Lemov splits the techniques into four main areas of checking for understanding (which correlates directly with Rosenshine), academic ethos, ratio and five principles of classroom culture, which also help support Rosenshine's principles.

Chris Moyse argues that observations should focus on one technique at a time and should be as long as is necessary in order to see it in practice, which may only be five or ten minutes. He also argues that when getting staff to observe peers selecting a staff member a year or two further into their career than the observer is more effective and far less intimidating than watching your most experienced outstanding practitioner. In reality the purpose of observations should only ever be to help the practitioner being observed or to learn from them by being the observer, never to catch people out. Chris talks a lot of sense that makes you wonder why we ever did anything different as a profession. *High challenge, low threat indeed.*

- **Urgently address under-performance. Prioritise staff not sharing the vision/values or with poor relations with pupils and other stakeholders.**

Teaching is a relationship-based profession and we know that poor pupil/ teacher relationships can be a risk factor in the development of mental health difficulties. Negativity and poor relationships are a huge potential drain on discretionary effort. It is difficult to create the right climate and culture when toxicity continues to thrive. It is always best to try to work with staff to help support them to understand the vision and values of the organisation, be it through training, mentoring or coaching, but ultimately, sooner or later, tough conversations may need to be had and difficult decisions made if the situation doesn't improve. Putting them off prolongs and exacerbates the situation and ultimately it is the young people who suffer. When this happens there is a moral imperative to act in their best interest as they only have one chance at school and we need to ensure it is as good as it can be. Offering an exit route that allows staff to leave with dignity, if it comes to it, and try to see if they can fit in elsewhere is the best solution for all concerned.

In order to achieve this, strong HR is required, unfortunately many schools – and now trusts – rely on local authority or ex-local authority staff in this respect. In my experience this can be a mistake. HR in local authorities often prioritises the limitation of reputational damage to the organisation rather than what is right for the children, school and often the member of staff concerned. Consequently, advice is overly conservative and strongly weighted toward staff rather than what is right or what is needed. When seeking HR support, they should prioritise what is right for the school by being solution focused and asking what outcome you want to see as a starting point. As a general rule, fast resolutions are more expensive than slower ones, but there is sometimes a need to move decisively and at speed for the good of the school and the children in it. Above all, when dealing with complex staffing issues make sure you follow advice to the letter as the only grounds to appeal a sanction are due to a procedural error, the fact that new evidence has come to light or that the sanction was unduly harsh. Seeking and heeding advice, therefore, is a prerequisite.

- **Understand risk and protective factors in relation to wellbeing and promote resilience, including mental health and attachment needs. Consider mental health first aid training.**

As we have seen, understanding the risk and protective factors for mental health difficulties is critical for helping shape staff understanding of unmet needs. Public Health England made a useful contribution to the debate by creating a graphic representation of the risk and protective factors, which though not as comprehensive as the DfE's list is much more user friendly for staff.

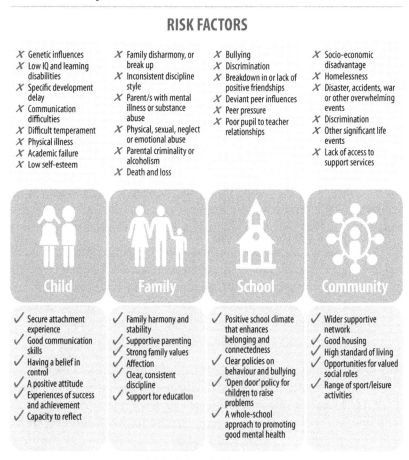

Figure 1: Risk and protective factors for children and young people's mental health by Public Health England, December 2016.

Lots of the risk factors are predictable, but breaking them down in to four areas allows us to really consider them. We have already discussed the impact of lack of communication difficulties, academic achievement and low self-esteem on mental health and we probably have some awareness that inconsistent discipline and bullying is damaging. It is unlikely that schools readily think of the isolated pupil who finds making and maintaining friendships in terms of their mental health. Similarly poor pupil teacher relationships, socio-economic disadvantage, discrimination and lack of access to services are all factors that schools needs to consider in relation to mental health.

The good news is that schools can mitigate these risks by strengthening the protective factors which is why we need to create time and space for reflection, promote consistency, have a positive culture and climate that build belonging and take a whole school approach to supporting mental health. Being able to promote valued social roles create easy wins for the busy teacher and the impact of sport and leisure activities cannot be overestimated. Exercise is critical in helping people of all ages feel better both physically and mentally and should always be encouraged. A range of activities at play times will increase the chances of young people getting involved as will after school clubs and school sports events and teams.

The Daily Mile is a no-cost solution that began in Scotland where by teachers take children out of class when they see fit to engage in 20 minutes of running three times a week. This may have benefits for some children with sensory issues and a number of regional coordinators have recently been appointed to support schools with implementation.

More information can be found on The Daily Mile website.

Some schools have used risk and protective factors proactively with staff to predict pupils who may be at risk through experiencing five or more of the risk factors and agree strategies to strengthen protective factors in mitigation. This is always a useful exercise to carry out with staff and resonates with the risks that may lead to mental illness, as captured by Lancet Psychiatry.

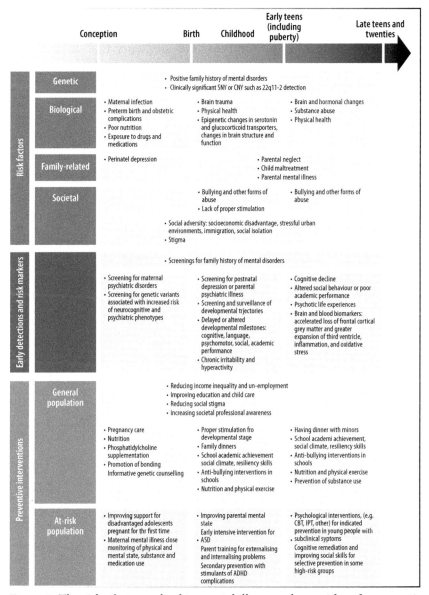

Figure 2: The risks that may lead to mental illness and some ideas for prevention from the Lancet Psychiatry as featured in The Guardian[2]

2. Rice-Oxley, M. (2019) 'Prevention: the new holy grail of treating mental illness', *The*

In turn, this overlaps with the publication 'Measuring and monitoring children and young people's mental wellbeing: A toolkit for schools and colleges', which also identifies four domains that inform such measurements. It goes on to give helpful suggestions for how to use tools to audit schools.[3]

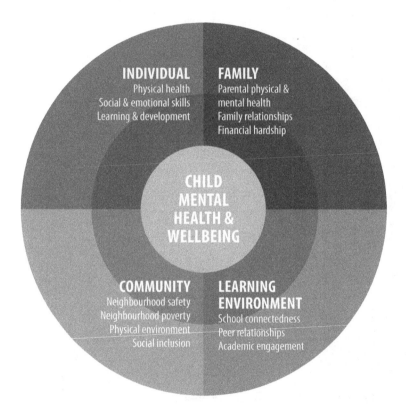

Figure 3: High-level domains that inform measurement of mental health and wellbeing[4]

Guardian [Online] 8 June. Retrieved from: www.bit.ly/2I2qfTC

3. Public Health England (No date) 'Measuring and monitoring children and young people's mental wellbeing'. Available at: www.bit.ly/2VBXkLD

4. Ibid.

- **Help staff understand, and pupils cope with, transition and change, including within the daily routine of school in order to make it predictable, remove uncertainty and reduce anxiety, e.g. movement between lessons, breaks, lunch, the start and the end of the day.**

Many schools only consider transition in relation to big movements in particularly between key stages and from primary to secondary school. Reframing transition as change can help staff understand that some children need to be supported when switching, either from one location to another or one task to another in order to curtail anxiety. Though should be given to all transitional point and times in the day. It doesn't need to be much but structure routine and consistency will help some children feel safe, emotionally contained and improve learning. Most children do not need such support but the ones that do will often be unknown to schools and be slipping behind in their learning. In one setting watching and discussing Newsround programme was introduced straight after lunch. This promoted consistency while also engaging children, expanding their worldview, improving their vocabulary and helping them make better sense of British values and the wider world. Story time, mindfulness/meditation sessions, prayer and reflection sessions can all be helpful aids to aid transition and promote a calmness, this is especially relevant for children who may live in chaotic circumstances.

- **Build staff understanding of child development, including neurological differences, incorporate environmental modifications and ensure systems successfully meet needs.**

We have discussed some neurological differences but staff should be aware of a wide range of conditions as what supports difference is often a refinement of good practice. Some staff consider modifications, such as visual timetables or having digital and analogue clocks, as somehow dumbing down, however it will not disadvantage those children that don't need it in any way while still supporting struggling learners. Those struggling will experience stress that, if continued, over time will lead to anxiety, which can lead to mental health difficulties.

Useful support for additional needs can be found through the NASEN SEND Gateway: www.sendgateway.org.uk

The Autism Education Trust: www.autismeducationtrust.org.uk

The National Autistic Society: www.autism.org.uk

MindEd (mental health support): www.minded.org.uk

YoungMinds (mental health support): www.youngminds.org.uk

The Anna Freud Centre (mental health): www.annafreud.org

The National Children's Bureau (advocacy): www.ncb.org.uk

The Communication Trust: www.thecommunicationtrust.org.uk

I Can (communication support): www.ican.org.uk

Dr Pooky Knightsmith (mental health): www.pookyknightsmith.com

The Charlie Wallar Memorial Trust (mental health): www.cwmt.org.uk

- **Create short, medium and long-term career plans for all staff and build in to professional growth cycle. Link to teachers' standards (see Appendix 6) and SEN code of practice.**

It is difficult to plan continuing professional development (CPD) and get the best out of staff if you don't know what they want to achieve in their career. Not everyone aspires to lead which presents great opportunities to train classroom practitioners to be the very best they can be. It is important to know who these staff members are and to develop their professional expertise as much as those who aspire to career progression. Similarly, if you know those that aspire to progress CPD can be planned and delivered accordingly at the appropriate time. All staff should be aware of the teachers standards and the SEN code of practice, both of which are useful to hold staff to account and can help support CPD.

- **Create tailored CPD for teaching and support staff to harness discretionary effort and empower appropriate individual career progression in line with school development plans.**

It seems obvious to say that CPD should be aligned to school improvement but this does not always happen. By using the framework and everyone being clear about the direction of travel, CPD can be powerfully used to support staff at every level by having a small number of improvement targets that multiple staff feed in to supporting. This should happen from CEO down in trusts and from head down in single or executive leaders role, e.g. when implementing the school improvement framework. Interestingly when we started talking to staff about specifics of career development those who were ambitious knew that they wanted to progress but few had given much thought to how they would do it. This approach forces staff to reflect on what they want to do, which allows milestones to be set. That isn't to say that they need to remain set in stone but understanding direction of travel and how it fits in to the school improvement framework is an effective way of driving discretionary effort as staff have greater ownership of their own development.

To that end we have worked hard to optimise our Apprenticeship Levy funding and have multiple teachers and support staff undertaking apprenticeship levy funded qualifications. The apprenticeship levy has given employers a whole new way to fund meaningful CPD but take up among trusts has been variable. After two years unspent apprenticeship levy is clawed back into treasury funding so it is imperative that schools investigate spending their levy lest they lose it.

In our trust we have developed an aspiring leaders course where 26 aspiring leaders from all seven of our schools come together over the course of a year for six three-hour sessions on a half termly basis. Each school nominates a senior leader who is responsible for supervising and supporting the other participants from their school as well as linking back to their SLT. In between each delivered session the aspiring leaders meet in their own schools to work through Leadership Matters by Andy Buck and complete their reflective journals ensuring a shared understanding of leadership. This concept stemmed from our experience of using a well-known provider to train middle leaders at great expense the previous year. While the content was good it was not bespoke to our context, nor did it result in any actual school improvement that could be measured to any meaningful extent, so we decided to do it ourselves and do it better.

Each participant in the course is required to research, plan and deliver an agreed strand of their school improvement plan for the following academic year informed by the framework intelligence gathering. Our intention is to run the course year on year to develop effective future leaders and will look into accreditation as an apprenticeship course so we can support other trusts with how to use the framework to drive school improvement at little or no cost the them. Schools who pay the levy can use it to fund training and those that don't only have to pay 10% of actual course costs (soon to decrease to 5%) if it is an accredited apprenticeship. This further acts to embed the framework while building capacity amongst senior and middle leaders.

Aspiring leaders course overview: Cohort 1

Objectives

- To improve pupil outcomes and protect emotional wellbeing of staff and pupils.
- To build capacity within schools and across the trust.
- To embed the school improvement model including common texts and approaches across the trust predicated on using research to inform practice.
- To support collaborative working across phases and sites.
- To use a range of data sources to drive bespoke improvement initiatives in each school.
- To deliver on key strands of the school improvement plan in the next academic year.
- To support staff aspiring to undertake the masters apprenticeship.

Who is eligible?

Staff must be self-motivated, committed to improving outcomes, hungry to learn by reading around their subject and be excellent classroom practitioners with clear leadership potential. Senior leaders (SLs) must be high performing and able to help supervise their aspiring leaders (ALs), both between sessions with their reflections on Leadership Matters and during the planning and delivery of their school improvement project, making links to the framework explicit. Both SLs and ALs should be open to using social media to inform their work and will need to bring a mobile device to each session.

What will it look like?

The course will require the pre-reading of the 'what works' framework. Core texts will include Leadership Matters and the reflective journal, which will be issued to all participants. Additional reading will be suggested and will be necessary to research the improvement projects.

The course will run from 12:30pm till 4pm on Wednesday afternoons, starting with lunch, subject to agreement and ratification of dates. It will comprise of six sessions over roughly one year so that aspiring leaders gain the skills and experience of planning and delivering a school improvement initiative. It is expected schools will nominate one senior leader and an agreed number of aspiring leaders, the SL will be the school contact point and be responsible for ensuring all surveys are planned for and delivered at the appropriate time. The proposed outline is as follows but may be subject to change:

Pre-course meeting with senior leaders to introduce their role and responsibility including materials, registration for Leadership Matters website and setting up a Twitter account. (Approximately one hour)

Session 1: Joining the dots on school improvement including introduction to leadership matters, MAT context and the school improvement framework in detail. Distribute *Leadership Matters* books and journals. **(November)**

Session 2: Moving from unconscious to conscious competence including introduction to the school improvement framework in detail, the impact of trauma on brain development and behaviour. **(January)**

Session 3: Building adult capacity to drive change including how to implement change, putting evidence to work. Where to find, and how to use, evidence to drive school improvement. **(March)**

Session 4: Planning a school improvement project using the framework and the outcomes from the questionnaires and standards audit including Individual presentations of proposed projects. **(June)**

Session 5: Seizing your authority as a leader and holding others to account and financial management. Including the fundamentals of HR, setting a budget, seeking additional funding and monitoring expenditure. **(October)**

Session 6: Reflecting on the school improvement journey so far. What worked well, what might be changed in the future and how do you know? Does anything we have learnt need to be built into the model in the future? **(Jan)**

Between each session reflective self-study will be set using the Leadership Matters video library, books and the reflective journals. Each session will begin with discussion based on the reflective Leadership Matters journals and will conclude by linking learning to future sessions and back to the framework. The course is intended to increase capacity in the trust and form part of our leadership pipeline by creating a pathway to apprenticeship masters courses focusing on the impact of improvement initiatives.

Successfully implemented school improvement projects that demonstrate impact may be incorporated into future iterations of the framework to ensure a culture of continuous improvement.

All participants will be expected to deliver a short presentation to governors at the end of their project focusing on the impact of their work.

Central team and support staff leadership training

We have also undertaken a leadership-training programme for our central team and support staff using Leadership Matters as a core text and based around the relevant parts of the school improvement framework so that those supporting schools share the same language and understanding of leadership creating greater consistency across the trust.

- **Keep abreast of new challenges and opportunities posed by technology.**

Technology is evolving at a faster pace than ever before and as a result schools need to remain technologically aware in order to safeguard children and take full advantage of new opportunities for learning. A few years ago the solution to all things IT was iPads and technology can be prone to expensive fads. These are best avoided and money invested instead on IT infrastructure. This is often overlooked in schools and as a result IT systems can become antiquated and potentially hinder learning. It is far better to have a clear on-going plan for IT development as by the time systems fall over the solution is usually prohibitively expensive to implement. Having high skilled, trusted technicians overseen by an experienced IT strategic lead who do not hide behind technical jargon and systems limitations is key to ensuring successful engagement with technology.

- **Develop robust induction programmes for all new staff including SEN protocols, behaviour systems, assessment and marking, vision and values, non-negotiables, and so on. Link to staff handbook.**

Robust induction is vital to ensure that new staff feel valued and optimise impact as soon as possible; having a staff handbook that outlines policies and procedures also helps prevent professional slippage. When things are going well, schools sometimes make the mistake of stopping doing the things that made things work well in the first place. An up-to-date staff handbook helps prevent this and acts as a default setting that can be returned to. It is also useful to help remind staff of standard operating procedures or the way we do things round here which that can be held to account for.

- **Use staff libraries of relevant CPD materials to inform the evidence base of what works.**

While staff should be encouraged to curate their own professional learning it is helpful for schools to hold staff libraries of relevant useful resources. This can be helpful to help shape staff thinking and discover which staff are serious about developing their learning. Subscription services such as The Key (www.thekeysupport.com) and The School Bus (www.theschoolbus.net) are relatively low cost additions to staff libraries offering almost unlimited support to any number of staff in schools. Forum Strategy also produce a subscription based, weekly briefing for MATs that is particularly useful, as well as organising regional networks and offering a range of other high quality strategic support services (www.forumstrategy.org).

Key learning

Use your contextual wisdom to build a coherent vision and set of values. Invite others to be part of it and to come on the journey, review it regularly to make sure it is still relevant.

Create a high challenge, low threat culture that encourages professional debate and challenge at all levels including among staff, governors, trustees and members.

Ensure all staff have access to high quality, evidence-based CPD that has an impact on raising standards.

Understand the risk and protective factors and use them proactively to inform practice and target vulnerable groups.

Robust induction programmes are vital for creating a sense of belonging and buy in from new starters at the earliest available opportunity.

Ensure staff are encouraged to think about their short, medium and long-term career plans so they can be supported to develop and benefit the school as they grow. Teachers who want to stay in the classroom should be helped through training and reflection to be the best teachers they can be.

What gets measured gets done so be clear on what you are measuring and why.

Make full use of your apprenticeship levy, even if you do not pay into it schools can access heavily discounted professional development.

Reflective audit

In answer to 'How well do we do this?', please give a single score to reflect where we are now based on:

1. Lack of consistent awareness among staff.
2. Some emerging awareness.
3. Increasing consistency with evidence of improving outcomes.
4. Embedded practices familiar to all staff and Included in staff handbooks and induction programmes. Staff routinely engage in professional dialogue to reflect on pupil learning and challenge orthodox thinking.

5. Strong evidence of embedded practice and improved outcomes. Senior leaders supporting in other settings.

In answer to priority please RAG rate based on:

Red = High priority

Amber = Medium priority

Green = Low priority

Adopt whole school inclusive thinking	How do you do this?/ What do you do?	How well does the school do this now? 1-5	How much of a priority is it? RAG rate	What actions might the school take?
Audit staff skill sets and ensure high quality, evidence-based CPD that addresses the needs of all stakeholders.				
Encourage staff at all levels to be professionally curious and engage in dialogue around relevant effective practice.				
Maintain accurate staff training registers ensuring training fits school development needs.				
Create bespoke improvement plans to enhance teaching and learning built on supporting staff to improve in a high challenge, low threat environment.				
Urgently address under-performance. Prioritise staff not sharing the vision/values or with poor relations with pupils and other stakeholders.				
Understand risk and protective factors in relation to wellbeing and promote resilience, including mental health and attachment needs.				

Adopt whole school inclusive thinking	How do you do this?/ What do you do?	How well does the school do this now? 1-5	How much of a priority is it? RAG rate	What actions might the school take?
Help staff understand, and pupils cope with, transition and change including within the daily routine of school, e.g. between lessons, breaks, lunch, start and end of day in order to make school predictable and reduce anxiety.				
Build staff understanding of child development, including neurological differences, incorporate environmental modifications and ensure systems successfully meet needs.				
Create short, medium and long-term career plans for all staff and build in to professional growth cycle. Link to teachers' standards and SEN code of practice.				
Create tailored CPD for all staff to harness discretionary effort and empower appropriate individual career progression in line with school development plans.				
Keep abreast of new challenges and opportunities posed by technology.				
Develop robust induction programmes for all new staff including SEN protocols, behaviour systems, assessment and marking, vision and values, standard operating procedures, and so on. Link to staff handbook.				
Use staff libraries of relevant CPD materials to inform the evidence base of what works.				

Potential action plan

Main priority areas (Low scoring and high priority)	Action needed	Evidence base	What will you do less of?	Link to Ofsted framework

Chapter 4
Developing supportive policies and procedures to promote consistency

'Consistency, structure and routine lead to outcomes far greater than the sum of their parts'.

– Me

- **Ensure that there are robust inclusive policies and practices in areas such as teaching and learning, safeguarding, behaviour, anti-bullying, e-safety and diversity, including tackling prejudice and stigma around mental health.**

Ensuring robust policies in place is really important in schools, especially when things go wrong because the first question asked will usually be 'can I see your policy on that please?' That is why policy and practice need to dovetail seamlessly – you could be answering similar questions in a court of law, an industrial tribunal or – perish the thought – a coroner's court.

Schools should have teaching and learning policies outlining their pedagogical model that includes not just the how but also the why. This should, of course, be drawn from a robust evidence base. We know the potential impact on mental health of things like bullying and stigma and it goes without saying they we need to keep young people safe. Anti-LGBTQ demonstrations outside schools in protest at compulsory sex

137

and relationship education are a vivid illustration of why schools have a moral duty to promote tolerance and respect difference.

A Public Health England blog post entitled 'Mental health challenges within the LGBT community' brought the need for support into sharp focus by pointing out:[1]

- Evidence suggests people identifying as LGBT are at higher risk of experiencing poor mental health.
- Members of the LGBT community are more likely to experience a range of mental health problems such as depression, suicidal thoughts, self-harm and alcohol and substance misuse.
- The higher prevalence of mental ill health among members of the LGBT community can be attributed to a range of factors such as discrimination, isolation and homophobia. This can lead to members of the LGBTQ community feeling dissatisfied with health services, with mental health services most often perceived to be discriminatory.
- It signposts support organisations for the LGBTQ community.

If you identify as LGBT and would like to talk to someone about your mental health, these organisations below may be a good place to start:

- Albert Kennedy Trust – supporting young LGBT people between 16 and 25 years old.
- Gendered Intelligence – working with the trans community and those who impact on trans lives with a particular focus on supporting young trans people under the age of 21.
- Imaan – the UK's leading LGBTQ Muslim charity.
- Stonewall and LGBT Consortium– services that enable you to find LGBT mental health services in your local area.

Before highlighting statistics that demonstrate the reality of the issue, namely:

- *52% of young LGBT people reported self-harm either recently or in the past compared to 25% of heterosexual non-trans young people*

---

1. Henderson, G. and Varney, J. (2017) 'Public health matters', *Public Health England* [Online] 6 July. Retrieved from: www.bit.ly/2u4n6MJ

and 44% of young LGBT people have considered suicide compared to 26% of heterosexual non-trans young people.

- *The Gay Men's Health Survey (2013) found that in the last year, 3% of gay men have attempted to take their own life. This increases to 5% of black and minority ethnic men, 5% of bisexual men and 7% of gay and bisexual men with a disability. In the same period, 0.4% of all men attempted to take their own life*

- *Prescription for Change (2008) found that in the last year, 5% of lesbians and bisexual women say they have attempted to take their own life. This increases to 7% of bisexual women, 7% of black and minority ethnic women and 10% of lesbians and bisexual women with a disability.*

- *The Trans Mental Health Study (2012) found that 11% of trans people had thought about ending their lives at some point in the last year and 33% had attempted to take their life more than once in their lifetime, 3% attempting suicide more than ten times.*

It concludes by noting that developing an LGBTQ inclusive approach to protecting and improving mental health and to prevent suicide should be done alongside LGBT community organisations and members.

- **Use strong local governance to draw on community strengths to provide challenge and support.**

Some trusts have dispensed with governance drawn from their local communities but we believe all communities have something to contribute. We conduct a skills audit of potential governors and ensure that our bodies are made up of suitably qualified professionals who can deliver challenge but we always ensure that this includes drawing on local community strengths. This also applies to MAT boards where care needs to be taken that the appropriate level of challenge is in place, especially where the boards have evolved from a single governing body or where long-standing relationships can lack rigor. This is particularly relevant for the CEO and the chair of trustees where good practice dictates a set period of office to prevent complacency, for example, on the London Stock Exchange, audit partners must be tendered for every ten years, though this is usually closer to five, and other changes are being discussed to further mitigate the potential for cosy relationships clouding judgments.

Boards should be eyes on and hands off other than at times of crisis. Governors and trust boards should help contribute to the vision and be able to articulate it in order to create collective efficacy.

In trusts there should be clear demarcation between members and trustees, as members have to hold trustees to account, lest they be accused of marking their own homework.

Steve Mumby, the ex-CEO of the National College, contrasts early high-profile multi-academy trust leaders with the current need to embrace imperfection. Those early leaders were often held up as being perfect, feted by politicians, with huge financial rewards and high public profiles culminating in the awarding of honours. For some it proved too much. They lost their ethical purpose and moral compass, particularly through lax recruitment and procurement processes. They felt untouchable and believed their own hype, awarding contracts to family members or close associates or employing them with insufficient regard to human resource protocols and employment law. More information on these cases is contained in an article by the TES from 2016.[2]

He argues that we need to embrace imperfect leaders who are open to the idea that they could make a mistake, thus opening themselves to external scrutiny and welcoming challenge to ensure it doesn't happen.

These cases highlight the impact of poor governance as, with the right checks and balances in place, such procedural irregularities would not have been able to happen as easily. Procurement is particularly susceptible to abuse if there is not a clear separation of duties. Schools should ensure that no one person accepts tenders for work and awards contracts as such an approach is open to abuse. It also leaves the member of staff vulnerable to allegations of wrongdoing. They should also ensure that staff contracts are awarded solely on merit and that close friends and relatives are not involved in the recruitment process at any stage. For the removal of doubt, anyone involved in any form of public office should ensure that they adhere to 'The Nolan Principles of Public Life', namely:

---

2. Vaughan, R. (2016) 'Charting the downfall of the "famous five" superheads'. *TES* [Online] 14 October. Available at: www.bit.ly/2IuFc0E

- **Selflessness**: Holders of public office should act solely in terms of the public interest. They should not do so in order to gain financial or other benefits for themselves, their family or their friends.
- **Integrity**: Holders of public office should not place themselves under any financial or other obligation to outside individuals or organisations that might seek to influence them in the performance of their official duties.
- **Objectivity**: In carrying out public business, including making public appointments, awarding contracts, or recommending individuals for rewards and benefits, holders of public office should make choices on merit.
- **Accountability**: Holders of public office are accountable for their decisions and actions to the public and must submit themselves to whatever scrutiny is appropriate to their office.
- **Openness**: Holders of public office should be as open as possible about all the decisions and actions they take. They should give reasons for their decisions and restrict information only when the wider public interest clearly demands.
- **Honesty**: Holders of public office have a duty to declare any private interests relating to their public duties and to take steps to resolve any conflicts arising in a way that protects the public interest.
- **Leadership**: Holders of public office should promote and support these principles by leadership and example.

Given that guidance on trust governance is continually evolving a credible external specialist such as the National Governance Association (NGA) should be engaged periodically to undertake reviews of both boards and local governance arrangements to ensure that governance at all levels remains relevant and effective. The NGA has recently launched an ethical leadership in education framework which draws on the Nolan Principles, while adding the personal characteristics or virtues required. More information and resources are available on the NGA website.

Forum Strategy, led by Michael Pain, can also advise boards and trusts, often forming rich, long-term relationships that provide critical rigor and challenge in a supportive manner. This really helps trusts to reflect on practice and drive improvements, while keeping up to date with the latest thinking in the field (www.forumstrategy.org).

We have recently altered the format of our local governing bodies to include presentations from middle leaders upwards at every meeting in a move away from only having heads reporting. This has supported more distributive leadership as staff have to be clear on what the issue is, what the evidence they propose to draw on to solve it is, what the impact will/ has been so far and what they needed to stop doing to make space for something new. This helps hold leaders at all levels to account, increases capacity, allows stress testing of the vision, values and pedagogical approaches and provide useful development for staff.

Academy Ambassadors (www.academyambassadors.org) can help trusts recruit board members and inspiring governance (www.inspiringgovernance.org) can support schools seeking to strengthen their local governance.

- **Use governor portal to facilitate transparent and effective governance, track progress between meetings and engender on-going professional dialogue.**

In an attempt at greater transparency and accountability, we have moved all governance documentation on to an e-portal. Our expectation is the all documentation is read online before any meeting, which has cut down on paperwork, served to track evidence of challenge from governors and boards and reduced the duration of meetings. Queries can be raised in advance via the portal and either addressed before meetings by senior leaders or prepared for dissemination in the meeting. This is more supportive for senior leaders and helps create space for other staff to present.

- **Ensure leaders at all levels are free to concentrate on teaching and learning and be both givers and receivers of support.**

A major plus point about operating within trusts or clusters is the opportunities offered for professional support of colleagues. We have a firm commitment to all schools being givers and receivers of support that means different skill sets and expertise can be identified and the impact shared across a range of settings rather than just one school. We have used this to good effect when supporting schools in their journey to good or better outcomes, but we also acknowledge that where schools are not yet good that they will contain areas of expertise that can be shared more widely. This has resulted in us appointing a senior leader to oversee safeguarding one day a week, another overseeing attendance for a day a week across the trust and two supporting teaching and learning.

- **Ensure staff handbook includes staffing structure, policies and procedures including teaching learning and assessment protocols to promote consistency. Review regularly to capture new initiatives and link to staff induction.**

As we have discussed, an up-to-date staff handbook is an essential part of preventing professional slippage and ensuring that policy and procedure do not drift apart. It is something that can date quickly, which seems to happen more readily in smaller schools with less capacity to keep on top of updating it. Relevant induction should be informed by the staff handbook so that new staff understand the culture and climate of the school they are joining and can contribute discretionary effort more quickly. This should be updated at least annually.

- **Further free up staff to concentrate on teaching and learning by devolving responsibility for fetes, discos, fundraising and so on to the local community supported by one named member of staff.**

Where schools are not running effectively they sometimes focus on the wrong things, rather than concentrating on improving outcomes, often because it seems like an overwhelming job that will require lots of hard work and difficult conversations. In these circumstances some leaders draw from the past and do lots of the nice to-dos rather than what is needed. The reality of this is the sooner you start, the sooner you finish, and by keeping what is right for children as the main thing then their life chances will improve, however this comes at a cost. Understanding your context and your personal dispositions as well at those of your team will help you to focus on the right things. This includes knowing the skill set of staff, what training they have or what they might need and then making a plan based on your knowledge of the school with improving teaching and learning at its core.

- **Ensure new initiative have the time and space to embed through a relentless focus on the objective and doing less of something else.**

Schools are very good at gathering pace by doing more and more 'stuff.' New initiatives often come along at a pace that is not practical or sustainable and that would not be attempted in other industries – especially without agreeing what staff will be required to stop doing to make way for any new practice. Constantly feeling that you are not on top of your job can engender negative thoughts that are damaging to staff wellbeing and impact on mental health. Unfortunately this strand scores poorly in virtually every school that has implemented the framework so it is essential that school leaders think carefully about what initiatives they implement and why, including what the evidence base is and how they fit alongside current practice. They then must decide what can be modified or stopped in order to make space for it to happen and change any relevant policies accordingly, which in turn needs to be reflected in the staff handbook and induction process.

Key learning

Promote the understanding and importance of the equality act to all stakeholders.

Use strong local governance to draw on community strengths but ensure relationships are not over comfortable and have sufficient rigor.

Ensure that a comprehensive staff handbook is maintained that gives a clear understanding of how you do things and why to eliminate professional slippage.

Schools must take time to embed new initiatives and do less of something else before doing something new in order to make workload manageable and avoid workload issues.

Consistency, structure and routine are greater than the sum of their parts. They make schools predictable and safe for pupils, reducing anxiety and improving results.

Reflective audit

In answer to 'How well do we do this?', please give a single score to reflect where we are now based on:

1. Lack of consistent awareness among staff.
2. Some emerging awareness.
3. Increasing consistency with evidence of improving outcomes.
4. Embedded practices familiar to all staff and Included in staff handbook and induction programmes. Staff routinely engage in professional dialogue to reflect on pupil learning and challenge orthodox thinking.
5. Strong evidence of embedded practice and improved outcomes. Senior leaders supporting in other settings.

In answer to priority please RAG rate based on:

Red = High priority

Amber = Medium priority

Green = Low priority

Adopt whole school inclusive thinking	How do you do this?/ What do you do?	How well does the school do this now? 1-5	How much of a priority is it? RAG rate	What actions might the school take?
Ensure that there are robust inclusive policies and practices in areas such as teaching and learning, safeguarding, behaviour, anti bullying, e-safety and dIversity, including tackling prejudice and stigma around mental health.				
Use strong local governance to draw on community strengths to provide challenge and support.				

Adopt whole school inclusive thinking	How do you do this?/ What do you do?	How well does the school do this now? 1-5	How much of a priority is it? RAG rate	What actions might the school take?
Ensure leaders at all levels are free to concentrate on teaching and learning and be both givers and receivers of support.				
Ensure staff handbook includes staffing structure, policies and procedures including teaching learning and assessment protocols to promote consistency. Review regularly to capture new initiatives and link to staff induction.				
Further free up staff to concentrate on teaching and learning by devolving responsibility for fetes, discos, fundraising, and so on, to the local community supported by one named member of staff.				
Ensure the voices of all stakeholders (pupils, parents, staff) are routinely captured to inform school improvement.				
Ensure when introducing a new initiative we make time and space for it to succeed through a relentless focus on the objective and doing less of something else				

Potential action plan

Main priority areas (Low scoring and high priority)	Action needed	Evidence base	What will you do less of?	Link to Ofsted framework

Chapter 5
Implementing targeted programmes and responses

'Ask yourself... who's not learning here?'

– Dale Bartle, educational psychologist

- **Ensure high quality implementation of specific learning programmes and interventions to address reduced progress that are proven to work.**

Often schools repeat the same intervention programmes time and time again without really stopping to question if they are effective. This may be because the school has invested in the resources; staff have had some training and may not want to change or both. This is potentially a false economy, once staff time is factored in interventions can be costly and schools need to be clear about the benefits of what they are doing or else seek out alternatives with a robust evidence base of success. Sometimes it may appear easier to do what has always been done but the outcomes are unlikely to change and it would be far better for children to do something different that is proven to work.

- **Be clear on intended outcomes and carefully monitor the impact of interventions.**

The only way schools can be sure of the impact of an intervention is if they are clear on what the intended outcomes are and then measure both start and finish points. Staff delivering them should be held to account for results, which should be monitored and validated to ensure accuracy and value for money.

- **Keep it simple and change what doesn't work.**

If the interventions are not proving effective schools should not be afraid to stop doing them. They need to consider if better value can be got from additional staff training, deploying them differently or if the intervention needs to change.

- **Explicitly teach social and emotional skills attitudes and values. Integrate this learning into the mainstream processes of school life. See: PSHE Association, PATHS, mental security and so on.**

We know that social and emotional skills are a better indicator of attainment and good leadership than IQ. We also know that children who have underdeveloped emotional skills for whatever reason are unlikely to suddenly develop them if we do not explicitly teach them. Social and emotional skills should be carefully planned and delivered linking with other pastoral opportunities in schools such as assemblies, registrations, reflection periods and so on. This links strongly with the culture and climate of the school, which is dictated by the leadership vision and values.

- **Ensure pupil interventions take account of non-academic needs, e.g. risk and protective factors for mental health difficulties, physical activities, sleep, diet, sense of belonging, strong adult relationships, that lay the foundations for academic achievement**

If the same children are undertaking interventions year on year then who is not learning? It may be time to consider other sorts of intervention focused more on strengthening the protective factors or looking at referrals for different forms of support, for example pastoral teams, heads of year/house.

Key learning

Ensure interventions are proven to work, carefully monitor impact and stop and change them if they don't work.

If you do what you have always done you will get what you have always got.

Remember emotional skills are a better indicator of academic attainment and leadership ability than intelligence quotient (IQ).

Explicitly teach social and emotional skills attitudes and values and be aware of the need for non-academic interventions to support learning for some children.

Always ask: 'who's not learning here?'

Reflective audit

In answer to 'How well do we do this?', please give a single score to reflect where we are now based on:

1. Lack of consistent awareness among staff.
2. Some emerging awareness.
3. Increasing consistency with evidence of improving outcomes.
4. Embedded practices familiar to all staff and Included in staff handbook and induction programmes. Staff routinely engage in professional dialogue to reflect on pupil learning and challenge orthodox thinking.
5. Strong evidence of embedded practice and improved outcomes and senior leaders supporting in other settings.

In answer to priority please RAG rate based on:

Red = High priority

Amber = Medium priority

Green = Low priority

Adopt whole school inclusive thinking	How do you do this?/ What do you do?	How well does the school do this now? 1 – 5	How much of a priority is it? RAG rate	What actions might the school take?
Ensure high quality implementation of specific learning programmes and interventions to address reduced progress and that are proven to work.				
Be clear on intended outcomes and carefully monitor the impact of interventions.				
Keep it simple and change what doesn't work.				
Explicitly teach social and emotional skills attitudes and values. Integrate this learning into the mainstream processes of school life. See: PSHE Association (www.psheassociation.org.uk), PATHS, mental security, and so on.				
Ensure pupil interventions take account of non-academic needs, e.g. risk and protective factors for mental health difficulties, physical activity, sense of belonging, and so on that lay the foundations for academic achievement.				

Potential action plan

Main priority areas (Low scoring and high priority)	Action needed	Evidence base	What will you do less of?	Link to Ofsted framework

Chapter 6
Implement targeted responses and identify specialist pathways

'The more healthy relationships a child has the more likely he will be to recover from trauma and thrive. Relationships are the agents of change and the most powerful therapy is human love.'

– *The Boy Who Was Raised as a Dog* by Bruce Parry.

- **Provide more intense work on social and emotional skill development for pupils in difficulties including one to one and group work.**

This part of the framework is very specific. It looks at what happens when interventions are unsuccessful and individual pupils continue to struggle. In those instances schools should seek to ensure more bespoke targeted responses are available – designed around individual needs. This might be via a tutor, pastoral team or external counselling service and should start by focusing on gaps in social and emotional skills.

- **Use specialist staff to initiate, innovative and deliver bespoke programmes to ensure they are implemented authentically then transfer responsibility to staff whenever possible to ensure sustainability and integration, for example SALT, OT, EP and so on.**

This will not be possible in all schools but where specialist support exists they should be used to train other staff to build capacity and offer supervision on an on-going basis. Such support is very expensive and usually demand will far outstrip supply so additional capacity allows a more tiered approach to support and allows for it to happen at the level of frequency necessary for it to be effective, rather than a weekly or bi-weekly session. These usually happen in isolation with staff often unsure of what has been done or achieved. Specialist staff should be used to audit staff skill sets, current practice and environments in order to identify training needs and build suitable whole school training programmes. Many schools now buy in counselling services for which there is an increasing and very necessary demand.

The national survey of children and young people's mental health by the NHS, published in 2018, revealed that more than one child in eight is experiencing a mental health difficulty, up from one in ten in 2004. It also stated: 'We know poverty, inequality and housing insecurity are closely linked with childhood mental health difficulties so we need to see concerted action to reduce these nationwide.'[1]

Coupled with a shortage of CAMHS (Child and Adolescent Mental Health Services) workers and skilled support, as well as a reduction in real term school funding, this is a potentially destructive combination for schools.

According to The Carnegie Centre of Excellence for Mental Health in Schools those with mental health needs are the group most likely to be eligible for free school meals, miss school, have the highest unauthorised absence rate and nearly 20% will have at least one school exclusion. This is the highest of any group and is likely to be for disruptive behaviour, or verbal and physical violence.

In October 2019 the Education Policy Institute released the 'Social Mobility & Vulnerable Learners' report that included research such as 'Unexplained pupil exits from schools: A growing problem?' in which they analysed data by trusts and local authority. What they discovered made for uncomfortable reading, especially when considering *which* pupils were more likely to experience an unexplained exit from school.

---

1. NHS (2018) *Mental Health of Children and Young People in England, 2017.* NHS [Online] 22 November. Retrieved from: www.bit.ly/2TAn0qy

They found that the overwhelming majority of unexplained exits – around three-quarters – are experienced by vulnerable pupils.

They include:

- Over 1 in 3 (36.2%) of all pupils who had also experienced a permanent exclusion.
- Around 1 in 3 (29.8%) of all looked after pupils (those in social care).
- Over 1 in 4 (27.0%) of all pupils with identified mental health needs (SEMH).
- Around 1 in 6 (15.6%) of all poorer pupils (those who have been on free school meals).
- Around 1 in 6 (15.7%) of all pupils with identified special educational needs (SEND).
- Around 1 in 7 (13.9%) of all pupils from black ethnic backgrounds.[2]

This raises interesting questions around ethical practices and gaming the system and, consequently, one of the preventative measures we have helped to create in response is the Mindful Healthcare Programme. This is a paid programme that can be part funded by pupil premium and provides online, collaborative support and recovery programmes for eight to 17-year olds and their families.

It brings families, schools and clinical practitioners together, to build resilience in young people and help them recover quickly from potential mental health problems.

The young person undertakes initial assessments and weekly online therapy sessions with the most appropriate qualified clinician to provide a bespoke response for those experiencing difficulties. Parents/carers and school are also offered advice on how to best support the young person to overcome their difficulties. This is being offered to any school/MAT in the UK and, through time, hopefully further afield.

More information can be found on the Mindful Healthcare website (www. mainfulhc.co)

---

2. Hutchinson, J. and Crenna-Jennings, W. (2019) 'Unexplained pupil exits from schools: Further analysis and data by multi-academy trust and local authority', in *Social Mobility & Vulnerable Learners*. Education Policy Institute. Retrieved from: www.bit.ly/2MusdNS

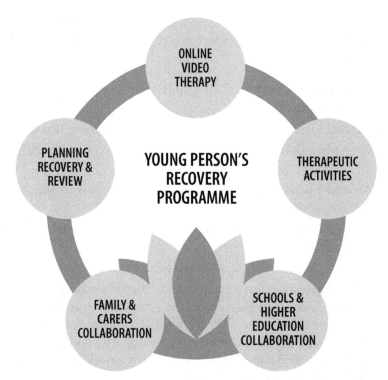

Figure 1: Mindful Healthcare recovery programme outline

One of the unintended outcomes of our Mindful trial was to uncover a number of highly concerning factors that only emerged due to clinical screening assessments. One school referred three Year 6 pupils to the programme only to discover from their parents during screening that two of them had experienced suicidal thoughts in the previous six-month period. Both had been turned down by CAMHS as being in need of support.

- **Ensure reasonable adjustments suggested above are known, understood and implemented faithfully by all staff through training and effective dissemination.**

Individual modifications are only effective when they are consistently applied which means that all staff need to know about them. Information needs to be disseminated in an effective way that ensures things do not slip between the cracks.

This is especially relevant when key staff change or at key transitional points, such as a new term or year. On-going monitoring of reasonable adjustments and training impact needs to be undertaken and refresher training added as and when needed to ensure effective implementation.

- **Where pupils experience difficulties, provide clear pathways for help and referral, using a coherent teamwork approach, including the involvement of outside agencies such as the NHS.**

Schools need to be clear about the process they go through to make a referral but they also need to know what to look for in relation to different difficulties. Additional needs should always be considered where young people exhibit behaviours that challenge or when learning slips further and further behind despite support.

- **Additional support for transitions are routinely accessed by those who need it, for example visual timetables, timers, personalised start and end of day routines, bespoke induction digital and analogue clocks in classrooms, and so on.**

This links with ensuring staff training and communication of information are both effective enough to ensure a consistently implemented approach to supporting the young person. The successes of such strategies are dependent on the strength of the weakest link on the team and ensuring they follow strategies faithfully.

One of our schools identified that in EYFS, pupils experienced 16 transitions in a morning that resulted in lots of time lost for learning and unsettled children. By reducing all but essential changes they have seen far greater engagement. They also added digital clocks as well as analogue ones to classrooms and turned off the highly obtrusive bells around the school. The result has been calmer children who are now all able to understand the time they have available to them to complete tasks, and work far more purposefully.

The school in our trust that has made the most progress in terms of therapeutic working has been Topcliffe Primary, which has a 60-place resource base for autism and speech, language and communication needs in a one-form entry school. They have long worked with speech and language therapists but last year added occupational therapy for half a day a week. Together with improvements identified by the framework and the dedication and deep thinking of the leadership team, the effects have been pronounced especially for pupils with additional needs.

SEN Headline Data 2017-2018

Key Stage 2 (Year 6):

Reading

	National 2018	Birmingham LA	All Inc RB 38	Mainstream 28	RB Only 10	Mainstream SEN Only 5	All SEN 15
Progress score of 0+	0	-0.3	3.4	2.4	6.85	10.1	7.99

Writing

	National 2018	Birmingham LA	All Inc RB 38	Mainstream 28	RB Only 10	Mainstream SEN Only 5	All SEN 15
Progress score of 0+	0	-0.4	3.0	2.1	5.91	7.52	6.48

Mathematics

	National 2018	Birmingham LA	All Inc RB 38	Mainstream 28	RB Only 10	Mainstream SEN Only 5	All SEN 15
Progress score of 0+	0	0.1	2.4	2.16	7.2	7.2	7.2

Figure 2: SEN headline data from Topcliffe Primary School

The average progress for SEND pupils across Birmingham in the same period was -1.9, yet here we see hugely accelerated gains despite different entry points for pupils in the resource base. Year on year exclusions have also fallen from 11 last year to only one this year, while attendance has increased.

Key learning

Ensure all staff are aware of reasonable adjustments to support learners needs. Sometimes they seem trivial but they can make a massive difference to young people. Not implementing them consistently is an overt rejection of the child and their needs, which will be counterproductive. Acceptance of them enhances belonging and lets the child know you care enough about them.

Support for individual young people experiencing difficulties can be provided by Mindful Healthcare (www.mindfulhc.co). Support should be sought at the earliest available opportunity to prevent difficulties developing into mental health problems.

Reflective audit

In answer to 'How well do we do this?', please give a single score to reflect where we are now based on:

1. Lack of consistent awareness among staff.
2. Some emerging awareness.
3. Increasing consistency with evidence of improving outcomes.
4. Embedded practices familiar to all staff and included in the staff handbook and induction programmes. Staff routinely engage in professional dialogue to reflect on pupil learning and challenge orthodox thinking.
5. Strong evidence of embedded practice and improved outcomes. Senior leaders supporting in other settings.

In answer to priority please RAG rate based on:

Red = High priority

Amber = Medium priority

Green = Low priority

Adopt whole school inclusive thinking	How do you do this?/ What do you do?	How well does the school do this now? 1-5	How much of a priority is it? RAG rate	What actions might the school take?
Provide more intense work on social and emotional skill development for pupils in difficulties including one to one and group work.				
Use specialist staff to initiate, innovative and deliver bespoke programmes to ensure they are implemented authentically then transfer responsibility to staff when-ever possible to ensure sustainability and integration, for example SALT, OT, EP and so on.				
Ensure reasonable adjustments suggested above are known, understood and implemented faithfully by all staff through training and effective dissemination.				
Where pupils experience difficulties, provide clear pathways for help and referral, using a coherent teamwork approach, including the involvement of outside agencies such as the NHS.				

Adopt whole school inclusive thinking	How do you do this?/ What do you do?	How well does the school do this now? 1-5	How much of a priority is it? RAG rate	What actions might the school take?
Additional support for transitions are routinely accessed by those who need it e.g. visual timetables, timers, personalised start and end of day routines, bespoke induction, digital and analogue clocks in classrooms, and so on.				

Potential action plan

Main priority areas (Low scoring and high priority)	Action needed	Evidence base	What will you do less of?	Link to Ofsted framework

Chapter 7
Connect appropriately with approaches to behaviour management[1]

'The child who is not embraced by the village
will burn it down to feel its warmth.'

– African Proverb

A recent Education Endowment Foundation (EEF) report found a lack of evidence to support zero tolerance behaviour policies, stating:

> ...today's report finds there is currently a lack of evidence looking at the impact of 'zero tolerance' policies as favoured by the DFE in recent years. Sometimes described as 'no excuses', these policies aim to create a strict and clear whole –school approach to discipline. Typically, under such policies pupils will automatically receive detention for a range of misbehaviours such as being late, forgetting homework or using rude language.[2]

Instead it suggests that regular routines such as meeting and greeting at the door and personalised responses are more effective but that consistency and coherence at a school level is paramount, which is fully in line with the framework.

---

1. With inspiration from *When the Adults Change, Everything Changes* by Paul Dix.
2. Education Endowment Foundation (2019) *Improving behaviour in schools guidance report*. London: Education Endowment Foundation. Retrieved from: www.bit.ly/2MxhLs7

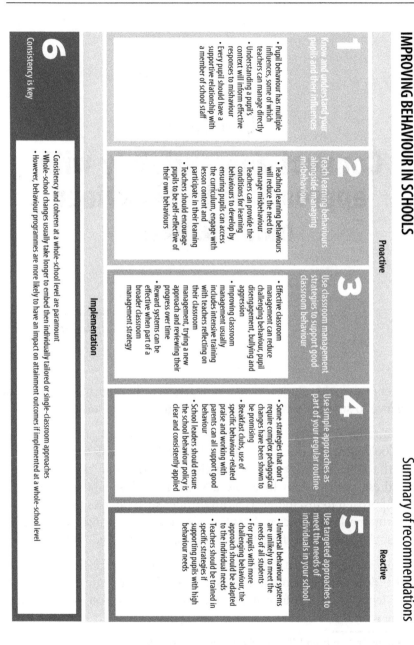

IMPROVING BEHAVIOUR IN SCHOOLS

Summary of recommendations

Proactive

1 Know and understand your pupils and their influences

- Pupil behaviour has multiple influences, some of which teachers can manage directly
- Understanding a pupil's context will inform effective responses to mishaviour
- Every pupil should have a supportive relationship with a member of school staff

2 Teach learning behaviours alongside managing misbehaviour

- Teaching learning behaviours will reduce the need to manage misbehaviour
- Teachers can provide the conditions for learning behaviours to develop by ensuring pupils can access the curriculum, engage with lesson content and participate in their learning
- Teachers should encourage pupils to be self-reflective of their own behaviours

3 Use classroom management strategies to support good classroom behaviour

- Effective classroom management can reduce challenging behaviour, pupil disengagement, bullying and aggression
- Improving classroom management usually includes intensive training with teachers reflecting on their classroom management, trying a new approach and reviewing their progress over time
- Reward systems can be effective when part of a broader classroom management strategy

Reactive

4 Use simple approaches as part of your regular routine to meet the needs of individuals in your school

- Some strategies that don't require complex pedagogical changes have been shown to be promising
- Breakfast clubs, use of specific behaviour-related praise and working with parents can all support good behaviour
- School leaders should ensure the school behaviour policy is clear and consistently applied

5 Use targeted approaches to meet the needs of individuals in your school

- Universal behaviour systems are unlikely to meet the needs of all students
- For pupils with more challenging behaviour, the approach should be adapted to the individual needs
- Teachers should be trained in specific strategies if supporting pupils with high behaviour needs

Implementation

6 Consistency is key

- Consistency and coherence at a whole-school level are paramount
- Whole-school changes usually take longer to embed then individually tailored or single-classroom approaches
- However, behaviour programmes are more likely to have an impact on attainment outcomes if implemented at a whole-school level

Figure 1: Summary of the EEF report into behaviour in schools

Charlie Taylor's behaviour checklist (see Appendix 7) also provides useful support.

- **Look upon 'difficult'/changed behaviour, reduced rate of academic progress or poor attendance/punctuality as a potential manifestation of unmet need/safeguarding issue.**

Reframing attention-seeking behaviours as attachment seeking is a powerful way to change staff thinking around individual children. In the same way, looking on difficult behaviours as a potential manifestation of unmet need is a powerful way to ensure a robust approach to both safeguarding and SEND.

Sudden change in school should be cause for immediate concern and treated as a potential safeguarding concern. If this takes place over the longer term it may still be a safeguarding issue but consideration should also be given to whether the child has an unmet need that needs to be investigated further rather than simply labelled as difficult.

The Timpson Review of School Exclusions in May 2019 found that 78% of pupils permanently excluded either have SEND, are classified as 'in need' or are eligible for free school meals.[3] 11% had all three characteristics. The zero tolerance narrative prevalent by some in the education debate risks further disadvantaging our most vulnerable pupils so all other opportunities for support should be fully explored at as early a point as is possible.

- **Respond actively with clear rewards and consequences for behaviour avoiding shame by offering a face-saving way out through restorative practice.**

Rewards should usually only be given for going over and above the norm. Children see straight through anything that is not consistently applied and equally fair for all. Too often schools focus on punishment that appears to driven from a desire to somehow extract revenge. For children struggling with deprivation, who may already have a punishing life, this is no way to teach belonging, compassion and love.

---

3. Department for Education (2019) *Timpson Review of School Exclusion.* London: The Stationery Office. Retrieved from: www.bit.ly/326onAQ

Paul Dix sums this up nicely: 'You can be strict without being nasty, maintain boundaries without cruelty and correct children without aggression.'[4]

- **Understand the deeper roots of lack of engagement, taking opportunities to model and teach positive alternatives.**

If pupils have poor social and emotional skills they will need to be supported to understand when they have made poor choices or disengaged from learning. To insist on an apology when young people may not have the same value system is counterproductive and will only generally result in resentment and a sense of shame. This will further reinforce any inner narrative the young person has about not being good enough, eroding belief in themselves as a learner and increasing stress.

It's far better for practitioners to take the opportunity to model what a more appropriate response might have been which also opens the door to using humour to improve mood. With some children acting out what a better scenario might look like helps give them an understanding of what they could do when facing the same situation in the future.

- **Closely monitor behaviour incidents including who, what, where, when and why and use data generated to spot patterns and build support plans.**

To be effective, behaviour data needs to record the right things and be analysed sufficiently to capture patterns. Always involve the child in unpicking what is wrong, check if all reasonable adjustments have been made and adhered to when incidents arise. Look at classes or times when the child does well and try to notice what is different and remember to consider the influence of others around them.

- **Use of consistent, calm adult behaviour by all staff.**

Humans have different levels of attunement to emotions and some vibrate like tuning forks in response to emotionally charged situations. This is why staff must have a consistent calm approach in order to support young people to co-regulate and bring their emotions under control.

---

4. Dix, P. (2017) *When the Adult Changes, Everything Changes: Seismic shifts in school behaviour*. Carmarthen, Wales: Independent Thinking Press.

This approach will prevent other tuning forks from picking up on the vibrations and explains why we needed to create the key 'be a leader not a follower' back in the SEMH schools.

- **Staff give first attention to best conduct, e.g. they focus on praising pupils making the right choices before dealing with those making the wrong choices.**

An important part of creating a positive culture and climate in schools is demonstrating what we value most highly in our schools. Focusing attention on those making the right choice sends a powerful message to everyone about what we hold dear. Poor choices should never be ignored but neither should the attention distract staff from what they intend to do.

- **Relentless, effective routines followed by staff and pupils.**

We know that some children will need more structured and routine ways of working than others. All children like and need structures and routines, without them some will become more anxious than others and heightened stress will result. In turn, this will inhibit ability to learn which is why everyone needs to understand and follow policies and procedures.

- **Scripted interventions used appropriately by all staff.**

We know that when stress is heightened a fight, flight or flock response can be triggered, which is why young people can find themselves caught up in an escalating spiral of argument if they are allowed to. There is also a danger of staff imposing their values on children who do not yet understand them before moving on. In order for staff to remain calm so that they can co-regulate the pupil, it is important they know exactly what to say and how to say it. This prevents young people playing adults off against each other and ensures a consistency that will help reassure all young people by preventing further escalation. This was something we achieved in the SEMH world through our Five Keys to Improvement (see Chapter 1).

- **Restorative follow up used by all staff to address behaviour incidents and improve relationships.**

Restorative practice is predicated on repairing and improving relationships once something has gone wrong. For children with poor social and emotional understanding, restorative approaches help them make sense of what to do next time without the detrimental impact on relationships that a solely punitive approach would engender. Hurt people and schools have a responsibility to break, not exacerbate that cycle.

- **Meet and greet successfully used by all staff to aid transitional times.**

Meeting and greeting at key transitional times can help build connectedness and a sense of belonging while actively scaffolding the transitions. This is particularly helpful for children living in challenging circumstances for whom the first smile or warm welcome at the start or end of a day might be the first or last they experience in a day. The sort of greeting will depend on knowing the context of the school and having an understanding of the individual children. It might be as simple as a nod, a simple smile or a more formal handshake.

> Indeed, long term and enduring changes to neural networks can be created by an intense period of stimulation that lasts less than a minute. Synaptic splitting – which is one way these connections can change – can occur in mere seconds of intense stimulation, and if the intense experience is repeated four times within an hour, the change will be maintained long term.

> Just as a traumatic experience can alter a life in an instant so too can a therapeutic encounter [...]. The good news is that anyone can help with this part of 'therapy' – it merely requires being present in social settings and being, well, basically, kind.

> An attentive, attuned, and responsive person will help create opportunities for a traumatized child to control the dose and pattern of rewiring their trauma-related associations. [...] The more we can provide each other these moment of simple, human connection – even a brief nod or a moment of eye contact – the more we'll be able to heal those who have suffered traumatic experience.[5]

5. Perry, B. (2017) *The Boy Who Was Raised as a Dog*. New York, NY: Basic Books.

- **Movements around school are ordered, calm and well managed especially at busy times. Pupils walk on the left and show courtesy to others.**

All staff need to understand their responsibility in helping ensure movements around school are ordered, calm and well-managed. In big schools support staff could help support between lessons in corridors, failure to do so can result in increased noise, escalating excitement and children arriving at their next lesson ill prepared to learn. Such times can increase anxiety in others and increase stress levels unnecessarily.

Our School Charter RRS

BE READY
- We arrive at school on time, every time.
- We get to lessons on time.
- We wear our uniform with pride and have the right clothes for PE and playing outdoors.
- We make sure we have the right equipment for all lessons.
- We take part fully in lessons and show resilience.

BE RESPECTFUL
- We always listen when an adult is talking.
- We are polite and show good manners to everyone.
- We respect difference and know we are all equal.
- We look after our equipment and share it.
- We look after our environment and never drop litter.
- We queue sensibly in the dining area and always tidy up.

BE SAFE
- We follow instructions - first time, every time.
- We stand up to bullying of any kind.
- We walk sensibly around our school.
- We know who to go to for help and support.
- We stay safe online and outside school.

Figure 2: Our School Charter at Firs Primary School

Key learning

Always look upon challenging or changes in behaviour as a cry for help or a potential manifestation of unmet need.

Avoid shaming children by reprimanding publicly where possible. Offer face-saving ways out through restorative practice. Do not accept poor behaviour nor let it go unchallenged but think carefully about how and when.

Create a culture where adults are calm and consistent in their approaches and do not insist on an apology before moving on.

Ensure relentless effective structures and routines are created by staff and followed by all pupils consistently.

Scaffold transitions through ordered calm movements and meeting and greeting pupils.

Reflective audit

In answer to 'How well do we do this?', please give a single score to reflect where we are now based on:

1. Lack of consistent awareness among staff.
2. Some emerging awareness.
3. Increasing consistency with evidence of improving outcomes.
4. Embedded practices familiar to all staff and Included in staff handbook and induction programmes. Staff routinely engage in professional dialogue to reflect on pupil learning and challenge orthodox thinking.
5. Strong evidence of embedded practice and improved outcomes. Senior leaders supporting in other settings.

In answer to priority please RAG rate based on:

Red = High priority

Amber = Medium priority

Green = Low priority

Adopt whole school inclusive thinking	How do you do this?/ What do you do?	How well does the school do this now? 1-5	How much of a priority is it? RAG rate	What actions might the school take?
Look upon 'difficult'/changed behaviour, reduced rate of academic progress or poor attendance/punctuality as a potential manifestation of unmet need/potential safeguarding issue.				
Respond actively with clear rewards and consequences for behaviour avoiding shame, which may become overwhelming by offering a face saving way out through restorative practice.				
Understand the deeper roots of lack of engagement, taking opportunities to model and teach positive alternatives.				
Closely monitor behaviour incidents including who, what, where, when and why and use data generated to spot patterns and build support plans.				
Use of consistent, calm adult behaviour by all staff.				
All staff give first attention to best conduct, for example they focus on pupils making the right choices before dealing with those making the wrong ones.				
Relentless, effective routines are followed by all staff and pupils.				

Adopt whole school inclusive thinking	How do you do this?/ What do you do?	How well does the school do this now? 1-5	How much of a priority is it? RAG rate	What actions might the school take?
Scripted interventions are used appropriately by all staff.				
Restorative follow up used by all staff to address behaviour incidents and improve relationships.				
Meet and greet successfully used by all staff to aid transitional times and build a sense of connectedness.				
Movements around school are ordered, calm and well managed especially at busy times. Pupils walk on the left and show courtesy to others.				

Potential action plan

Main priority areas (Low scoring and high priority)	Action needed	Evidence base	What will you do less of?	Link to Ofsted framework

Main priority areas (Low scoring and high priority)	Action needed	Evidence base	What will you do less of?	Link to Ofsted framework

Chapter 8
In conclusion

*'Develop resilience and be brave. There are days when it is very
discouraging. You have to develop personal resilience to environmental
things that come along. If you let every single environmental challenge
knock you off your game, it's going to be very, very hard.'*

– Renee James

A rising tide lifts all the boats

The emotional wellbeing school improvement framework is designed
to continuously improve schools over time. Once elements of the
framework are embedded, they will act as a rising tide, ensuring
each constituent part lifts higher as understanding and capacity are
developed. Some low hanging fruit can be picked quickly and easily but
it will then take a patient approach. A reliance on research, contextual
wisdom and the support of a range of disciplines will ensure progress is
sustained and meaningful, as long as embedding the framework is made
the responsibility of leaders at all levels.

The six tools that every leader needs to be effective

David Carter made a valuable contribution to the leadership debate when
he publicised his leadership toolkit, which should be used to stress test
any school improvement plans. He began by asking what the leadership
challenges facing education were currently and outlining seven key areas:

- To do more with less.
- To convince graduates that teaching is the career for them.
- To create better educational opportunities for all children, but especially those who are vulnerable.
- To build the mental wellbeing of the system from the classroom up.
- To take more notice of research and evidence-based thinking.
- To play a leading role in delivering greater social mobility in a fairer way than ever before.
- Better progression into the workplace with young people who blend skills with aptitude and great attitudes.

He then went on to look at the personal characteristics that the leaders of tomorrow will need:

- To build their strategy upon solid research and evidence of what it is that works.
- Have emotional mastery of the key change management moments as well as knowing what to do.
- How does it feel to lead this change?
- Strong self-awareness traits that reflect personal strengths and vulnerabilities: 'What is it like to be led by me?'
- A belief in ethical and morally driven decision making.
- Take decisions that adds capacity to your community rather than taking it away.
- Cope with setbacks and difficulties whilst staying focused and purposeful.

What that would look like in terms of professional characteristics:

- These six characteristics are already being nurtured, but we only see how important they are when we cannot find them in our toolkits:
  - Knowing why we are going to do something.
  - Knowing how we are going to do it.
  - Knowing what we are going to do.
  - Knowing when to do it.

- Knowing which strategy to set.
- Knowing who to communicate with.

Before outlining the six tools that would help achieve it all:

Tool 1: Knowing *why* we are going to do something (moral purpose and values)

Clarity of purpose and making sense of change means that **knowing why** we are doing something is critical.

Four questions our colleagues now, and in the future, are entitled to ask:

- What is the core purpose of the change we are preparing for?
- How does the change relate to the moral purpose of the school or organisation I work for?
- Who is going to tell me what my role in this is going to be?
- Who will tell me if I have performed well?

Tool 2: Knowing *when* we are going to do it (timing and execution)

Being clear about **knowing when** the timing of leadership change making is critical to the credibility of the leader.

Four questions our colleagues now and in the future are entitled to ask:

- If we are going to do something new what will we do less of?
- How long will it take to implement the change?
- How much time will we devote to preparing staff to work differently?
- How will we tell children, families and carers what we are going to do?

Tool 3: Knowing *what* we are going to do (action and delivery)

Knowing what the expectations are of each individual is fundamental to leaders being successful. Four questions our colleagues now and in the future are entitled to ask:

- What are the goals of the change?

- What will we achieve in the short term to know we are on track to achieving our goal?
- Can we afford to deliver this new priority?
- What are the opportunity costs of proceeding?

Tool 4: Knowing *how* we are going to do it (leading collaboration)

Knowing how the leadership of change will be managed will be critical to the credibility of the leader.

Four questions our colleagues now and in the future are entitled to ask:

- How will we learn from the work of others so that we are evidence led?
- How will our practice evolve to be more effective than it is today?
- How will we know we are on track to be successful?
- How will we be responsive to feedback as our change plans evolve?

Tool 5: Knowing *which* strategy to set (vision to reality)

Knowing which strategy to place at the core of the change process is critical to the success of the implementation process and the credibility of the leader.

Four questions our colleagues now and in the future are entitled to ask:

- How easy is it to describe the vision we are trying to reach?
- How will we define the roles of the different leaders and members of the workforce in the change process?
- How clear is the timeline to delivery?
- How will we monitor the impact of the change?

Tool 6: Knowing *who* to communicate with (engagement and followship)

Knowing who to communicate with and **when** is a critical part of the change process. Building a coalition of support through engagement builds fellowship and commitment.

Four questions our colleagues now and in the future are entitled to ask:

- How do I provide feedback on my personal experience of change?
- How can I better understand the detail of the change so that I can explain it to my team members?
- How will we record the process for future learning?
- How will we ensure that we learn about what is not working as well as that which is?

Finally, David Carter asked how do the leaders of today ensure that the leaders of tomorrow are equipped to be even more effective than we have been? How do they pass the jersey on stronger? This is precisely what embedding the emotional wellbeing school improvement framework will do by protecting emotional wellbeing while maximising learning outcomes.

Future developments

As of September 2019 we have created a therapeutic team consisting of an educational psychologist, a team of speech and language therapists and an occupational therapist . We have identified therapeutic champions in each setting who will be trained to screen pupils and deliver interventions under the supervision of the therapists. The therapists will also audit environments and skills to identify gaps in practice or training and lead whole school CPD accordingly.

We will work with our EPs to refine the framework further. We are also creating an aspiring leaders equivalent course focusing on leadership for support staff and developing a career development pledge that will identify opportunities for staff at all levels.

We will begin our second aspiring leaders cohort, which will build further capacity in the trust and seek an external partner to help accredit the course so it can become available as an apprenticeship and qualify for levy funding. This will enable us to train other schools/trusts in leadership through using the framework to drive school improvement at no additional cost to them other than time out of school.

We will explore the creation of an electronic platform to host survey data and provide resources to support the implementation of the framework and will be looking to roll out our Mindful programme to schools and universities for those who cannot get clinical support for their young people and will include the views of our new therapeutic team in the next iteration of the framework.

Additionally, we will seek to further embed our framework, as we know structures and routines need time to embed for both staff and pupils in order to create consistency. To do this we will work to involve wider staff teams including governors and trustees while supporting schools where engagement with the process has been less effective so that everyone understands the way we do things, and to that end we have organised a visioning day for trustees, heads and directors, organised a whole MAT training day on restorative practices, and began an ambitious plan to upskill staff in therapeutic support designed to support all children achieve, not just those with additional needs.

Above all, we will continue to act with integrity, behave with humility, treat people with compassion and work in the best interest of those we serve at all times. This will enable us to develop trust and help really build belonging in order to create brighter futures for our children and healthier, happier workplaces for our staff.

Appendix 1
Teaching and learning survey

NB This is best done over two sessions

Emotional wellbeing school improvement plan staff audit tool

(To be used in conjunction with the emotional wellbeing school improvement framework)

In answer to 'How well do we do this?', please give a single score to reflect where we are now based on:

1. Lack of consistent awareness among staff.
2. Some emerging awareness.
3. Increasing consistency with evidence of improving outcomes.
4. Embedded practices familiar to all staff and included in staff handbook and induction programmes. Staff routinely engage in professional dialogue to reflect on pupil learning and challenge orthodox thinking.
5. Strong evidence of embedded practice and improved outcomes. Senior leaders supporting in other settings.

The lowest scoring areas should inform potential lines of enquiry for the school improvement plan in terms of specific objectives and next steps. The highest scoring areas are potential strengths to inform the school self-assessment form. Both should be triangulated with pupil and parent surveys, as well as the quality assurance audit.

Adopt whole school inclusive thinking (Emphasis on consistency being key)	How well does the school do this? 1-5	Comments
Use whole school approaches to create alignment based on clear vision, values and non-negotiables to foster consistent structures and routines that support teaching and learning, remove unnecessary distractions and link financial planning to school improvement.		
Promote a relentless focus on high aspirations and improving teaching and learning through a knowledge-based curriculum that meets the needs of all pupils.		
Ensure all staff understand their individual and collective responsibility for improving outcomes in an outward looking, solution focused, safeguarding centred culture.		
Leaders at all levels should model empathy and resilience, demonstrating emotional intelligence and positivity especially in the most challenging circumstances. Work should have a sense of urgency and purpose.		
Create clearly defined staffing structures with precisely defined roles and responsibilities. Align them to effective job descriptions that support delivery of the school development plan.		
Ensure accuracy of judgments through moderation, triangulation and benchmarking and use it as a coaching opportunity to drive improvements.		
Take time to fully embed new initiatives and avoid initiative overload.		

Adopt whole school inclusive thinking (Emphasis on consistency being key)	How well does the school do this? 1-5	Comments
Promote wellbeing to help prevent problems and improve self-esteem by creating time for reflection to promote positive attitudes.		
Emphasise the acceptance of emotion, respect, warm relationships and celebrate difference.		
Research evidence base of what works effectively to improve outcomes, visit other settings. See: The Education Endowment Foundation, What Works Centre for Wellbeing, ResearchEd, Chartered College, Doug Lemov, Hattie, and so on.		
Promote staff wellbeing and particularly address staff stress levels including a healthy life work balance and boundaried working practices.		
Engage proactively with families to forge positive relationships, a sense of belonging and work in the best interests of children		

Prioritise professional learning and staff development	How well? 1-5	Comments
Audit staff skill sets and ensure high quality, evidence-based CPD that addresses the needs of all stakeholders.		
Encourage staff at all levels to be professionally curious and engage in dialogue around relevant effective practice.		
Maintain accurate staff training registers ensuring training fits school development needs.		
Create bespoke improvement plans to enhance teaching and learning built on supporting staff to improve in a high challenge low threat environment		
Urgently address under-performance. Prioritise staff not sharing the vision/values or with poor relations with pupils and other stakeholders.		
Understand risk and protective factors in relation to wellbeing and promote resilience including mental health and attachment needs.		
Help staff understand, and pupils cope with transition and change including within the daily routine of school e.g. between lessons, breaks, lunch, the start and the end of the day in order to make school predictable and reduce anxiety.		

Prioritise professional learning and staff development	How well? 1-5	Comments
Build staff understanding of child development, including neurological differences, incorporate environmental modifications and ensure systems successfully meet needs.		
Create short, medium and long-term career plans for all staff and build in to professional growth cycle. Link to Teachers' Standards and SEN code of practice.		
Create tailored CPD for all staff to harness discretionary effort and empower appropriate individual career progression in line with school development plans.		
Keep abreast of new challenges and opportunities posed by technology.		
Develop robust induction programmes for all new staff including SEN protocols, behaviour systems, assessment and marking, vision and values, standard operating procedures etc. Link to staff handbook.		
Use staff libraries of relevant CPD materials to inform the evidence base of what works.		

Develop supportive policies/procedure (promoting consistency)	How well? 1-5	Comments
Ensure that there are robust inclusive policies and practices in areas such as teaching and learning, safeguarding, behaviour, anti bullying, e-safety and diversity, including tackling prejudice and stigma around mental health.		
Use strong local governance to draw on community strengths to provide challenge and support.		
Ensure Leaders at all levels are free to concentrate on teaching and learning and be both givers and receivers of support.		
Ensure staff handbook includes staffing structure, policies and procedures including teaching learning and assessment protocols to promote consistency. Review regularly to capture new initiatives and link to staff induction.		
Further free up staff to concentrate on teaching and learning by devolving responsibility for fetes, discos, fund raising etc. to the local community supported by one named member of staff.		
Ensure the voices of all stakeholders (pupils, parents, staff) are routinely captured to inform school improvement.		
Ensure when introducing a new initiative we make time and space for it to succeed through a relentless focus on the objective and doing less of something else		

Develop supportive policies/procedure (promoting consistency)	How well? 1-5	Comments
IT systems are fit for purpose and help improve teaching and learning.		

Implement targeted programmes and interventions (including curriculum)	How well? 1-5	Comments
Ensure high quality implementation of specific learning programmes and interventions to address reduced progress and that are proven to work.		
Be clear on intended outcomes and carefully monitor the impact of interventions.		
Keep it simple and change what doesn't work.		
Explicitly teach social and emotional skills attitudes and values. Integrate this learning into the mainstream processes of school life. See: PSHE Association (www.psheassociation. org.uk), mental security, and so on.		
Ensure pupil interventions also take account of non-academic needs where necessary, for example risk and protective factors for mental health difficulties, physical activity, sense of belonging that lay the foundations for academic achievement.		

Implement targeted responses and identify specialist pathways (including therapeutic)	How well? 1-5	Comments
Provide more intense work on social and emotional skill development for pupils in difficulties including one to one and group work.		
Use specialist staff to initiate, innovative and deliver bespoke programmes to ensure they are implemented authentically then transfer responsibility to staff when-ever possible to ensure sustainability and integration, for example SALT, OT, EP, and so on.		
Ensure reasonable adjustments suggested above are known, understood and implemented faithfully by all staff through training and effective dissemination.		
Where pupils experience difficulties, provide clear pathways for help and referral, using a coherent teamwork approach, including the involvement of outside agencies such as the NHS.		
Additional support for transitions are routinely accessed by those who need it e.g. visual timetables, timers, personalised start and end of day routines, bespoke induction, digital and analogue clocks in classrooms, and so on.		

Connect appropriately with approaches to behaviour management	How well? 1-5	Comments
Look upon 'difficult' /changed behaviour, reduced rate of academic progress or poor attendance/punctuality as a potential manifestation of unmet need/ safeguarding issue.		

Connect appropriately with approaches to behaviour management	How well? 1-5	Comments
Respond actively with clear rewards and consequences for behaviour avoiding shame, which may become overwhelming by offering a face saving way out through restorative practice.		
Understand the deeper roots of lack of engagement, taking opportunities to model and teach positive alternatives.		
Closely monitor behaviour incidents including who, what, where, when and why and use data generated to spot patterns and build support plans.		
Ensure use of consistent, calm adult behaviour by all staff.		
All Staff give first attention to best conduct, for example they focus on pupils making the right choices before dealing with those making the wrong ones.		
Relentless, effective routines are followed by all staff and pupils.		
Scripted interventions are used appropriately by all staff.		

Connect appropriately with approaches to behaviour management	How well? 1-5	Comments
Restorative follow up used by all staff to address behaviour incidents and improve relationships.		
Meet and greet successfully used by all staff to aid transitional times and build a sense of connectedness.		
Movements around school are ordered, calm and well managed especially at busy times. Pupils walk on the left and show courtesy to others.		

Appendix 2
Pupil survey

Class _____

	Statement	1 Strongly disagree	2 Disagree	3 Agree	4 Strongly agree
1	I feel I belong in my school				
2	Work is interesting and challenging				
3	I sometimes find work too easy				
4	Teachers' explanations are clear and easy to follow				
5	Teachers encourage me to speak in class				
6	I know what lessons I am going to have each day				
7	I get help when I need it				
8	Homework helps improve my learning				
9	Staff feedback helps me improve my work				
10	There is a friendly atmosphere in our school				
11	I worry about getting things wrong				
12	I know what I need to do to improve my work				
13	I feel I belong in my school				

	Statement	1 Strongly disagree	2 Disagree	3 Agree	4 Strongly agree
14	Adults in school are always calm , consistent and friendly				
15	Staff praise good choices by pupils before they focus on those making bad choices				
16	Behaviour in my school is good				
17	Staff meet and greet me at the start of class				
18	Movements around school are calm and well managed				
19	Technology in school helps improve my learning				
20	I know my views are valued in school				
21	I get enough opportunities to exercise at school				

22	What do you think makes a lesson good? Write down your ideas below. **The key ingredients for a good lesson are...**
23	What can make it hard for you to learn? Write down here what you think below. **It can be hard to learn when...**

24	What do you like most about your school?
25	What would you most like to improve about your school?

Thank you for taking time to complete this survey. We will listen carefully to what you tell us and work hard to help improve your school.

Appendix 3
Parent survey

This survey will be used together with pupil and staff surveys to inform school improvement themes for the next academic year. Surveys will be completed anonymously and will be analysed by senior staff.

Please circle a number for each statement, according to the following key: 1. Strongly disagree 2. Disagree 3. Agree 4. Strongly agree				
I am clear about the school's vision and values	1	2	3	4
The school has high aspirations for all pupils and encourages them to achieve their best	1	2	3	4
The school is welcoming and builds good relationships with families and carers	1	2	3	4
My child is happy at this school	1	2	3	4
My child feels safe at this school	1	2	3	4
My child makes good progress at this school	1	2	3	4
Homework helps improve my child's learning	1	2	3	4

Please circle a number for each statement, according to the following key: 1. Strongly disagree 2. Disagree 3. Agree 4. Strongly agree				
This school makes sure its pupils are well behaved	1	2	3	4
This school deals effectively with bullying	1	2	3	4
This school is well led and managed	1	2	3	4
This school responds well to any concerns I raise	1	2	3	4
I receive valuable information from the school about my child's progress	1	2	3	4
My child gets enough opportunities to exercise at this school	1	2	3	4

What are the school's greatest strengths?

What could the school improve?

If you wish, please add any further comments that you feel would be helpful

Thank you for completing this survey. If you wish, please include your name below.

Name: _____

Appendix 4
Support staff survey

Adopt whole school inclusive thinking (emphasis on consistency being key)	How well does the school do this? 1-5	Comments
Use whole school approaches to create alignment based on clear vision, values and non-negotiables.		
Ensure all staff understand their individual and collective responsibility for improving outcomes in an outward looking, solution focused, safeguarding centred culture.		
Leaders at all levels should model empathy and resilience, demonstrating emotional intelligence and positivity especially in the most challenging circumstances. Work should have a sense of urgency and purpose.		
Create clearly defined staffing structures with precisely defined roles and responsibilities. Align them to effective job descriptions that support delivery of the school development plan.		
Take time to fully embed new initiatives and avoid initiative overload.		

Adopt whole school inclusive thinking (emphasis on consistency being key)	How well does the school do this? 1-5	Comments
Promote wellbeing to help prevent problems and improve self-esteem by creating time for reflection to promote positive attitudes.		
Emphasise the acceptance of emotion, respect, warm relationships and celebrate difference.		
Promote staff wellbeing and particularly address staff stress levels including a healthy life work balance and boundaried working practices.		
Engage proactively with families to forge positive relationships, a sense of belonging and work in the best interests of children.		

Prioritise professional learning and staff development	How well? 1-5	Comments
Audit staff skill sets and ensure high quality evidence based CPD that addresses the needs of all stakeholders.		
Encourage staff at all levels to be professionally curious and engage in dialogue around relevant effective practice.		
Urgently address under-performance. Prioritise staff not sharing the vision/values or with poor relations with pupils and other stakeholders.		
Create short, medium and long-term career plans for all staff and build in to professional growth cycle.		
Create tailored CPD for all staff to harness discretionary effort and empower appropriate individual career progression in line with school development plans.		
Keep abreast of new challenges and opportunities posed by technology.		
Develop robust induction programmes for all new staff including SEN protocols, behaviour systems, assessment and marking, vision and values, standard operating procedures etc. Link to staff handbook.		

Develop supportive policies/procedure (promoting consistency)	How well? 1-5	Comments
Ensure that there are robust inclusive policies and practices in areas such as teaching and learning, safeguarding, behaviour, anti bullying, e-safety and diversity, including tackling prejudice and stigma around mental health.		
Ensure staff handbook includes staffing structure, policies and procedures including teaching learning and assessment protocols to promote consistency. Review regularly to capture new initiatives and link to staff induction.		
Ensure the voices of all stakeholders (pupils, parents, staff) are routinely captured to inform school improvement.		
Ensure when introducing a new initiative we make time and space for it to succeed through a relentless focus on the objective and doing less of something else		
IT systems are fit for purpose and help improve teaching and learning.		

Connect appropriately with approaches to behaviour management	How well? 1-5	Comments
Look upon 'difficult' /changed behaviour, reduced rate of academic progress or poor attendance/punctuality as a potential manifestation of unmet need/safeguarding issue.		
Ensure use of consistent, calm adult behaviour by all staff.		
All staff give first attention to best conduct, for example they focus on pupils making the right choices before dealing with those making the wrong ones.		
Relentless, effective routines are followed by all staff and pupils.		
Movements around school are ordered, calm and well managed, especially at busy times. Pupils walk on the left and show courtesy to others.		

Appendix 5
School improvement framework data overview

School name _____

Evidence source	Strengths	Areas for development
Staff survey		
Pupil questionnaire		

Evidence source	Strengths	Areas for development
Parent questionnaire		
Quality assurance visit		

School improvement plan objectives agreed

Any barriers to completing the process?

Any changes or improvements needed for next year?

Any other comments/observations?

Appendix 6
National standards of excellence for headteachers

The four domains

The *national standards of excellence for headteachers* are set out in four domains, beginning with a preamble. There are four 'excellence as standard' domains:

- Qualities and knowledge
- Pupils and staff
- Systems and process
- The self-improving school system

Within each domain there are six key characteristics expected of the nation's headteachers.

Domain one
Excellent headteachers: qualities and knowledge

Headteachers:

1. Hold and articulate clear values and moral purpose, focused on providing a world-class education for the pupils they serve.
2. Demonstrate optimistic personal behaviour, positive relationships and attitudes towards their pupils and staff, and towards parents, governors and members of the local community.

3. Lead by example – with integrity, creativity, resilience, and clarity – drawing on their own scholarship, expertise and skills, and that of those around them.

4. Sustain wide, current knowledge and understanding of education and school systems locally, nationally and globally, and pursue continuous professional development.

5. Work with political and financial astuteness, within a clear set of principles centred on the school's vision, ably translating local and national policy into the school's context.

6. Communicate compellingly the school's vision and drive the strategic leadership, empowering all pupils and staff to excel.

Domain two

Excellent headteachers: pupils and staff

Headteachers:

1. Demand ambitious standards for all pupils, overcoming disadvantage and advancing equality, instilling a strong sense of accountability in staff for the impact of their work on pupils' outcomes.

2. Secure excellent teaching through an analytical understanding of how pupils learn and of the core features of successful classroom practice and curriculum design, leading to rich curriculum opportunities and pupils' wellbeing.

3. Establish an educational culture of 'open classrooms' as a basis for sharing best practice within and between schools, drawing on and conducting relevant research and robust data analysis.

4. Create an ethos within which all staff are motivated and supported to develop their own skills and subject knowledge, and to support each other.

5. Identify emerging talents, coaching current and aspiring leaders in a climate where excellence is the standard, leading to clear succession planning.

6. Hold all staff to account for their professional conduct and practice.

Domain three

Excellent headteachers: systems and process

Headteachers:

1. Ensure that the school's systems, organisation and processes are well considered, efficient and fit for purpose, upholding the principles of transparency, integrity and probity.
2. Provide a safe, calm and well-ordered environment for all pupils and staff, focused on safeguarding pupils and developing their exemplary behaviour in school and in the wider society.
3. Establish rigorous, fair and transparent systems and measures for managing the performance of all staff, addressing any under-performance, supporting staff to improve and valuing excellent practice.
4. Welcome strong governance and actively support the governing board to understand its role and deliver its functions effectively – in particular its functions to set school strategy and hold the headteacher to account for pupil, staff and financial performance.
5. Exercise strategic, curriculum-led financial planning to ensure the equitable deployment of budgets and resources, in the best interests of pupils' achievements and the school's sustainability.
6. Distribute leadership throughout the organisation, forging teams of colleagues who have distinct roles and responsibilities and hold each other to account for their decision-making.

Domain four

Excellent headteachers: the self-improving school system

Headteachers:

1. Create outward-facing schools, which work with other schools and organisations – in a climate of mutual challenge – to champion best practice and secure excellent achievements for all pupils.

2. Develop effective relationships with fellow professionals and colleagues in other public services to improve academic and social outcomes for all pupils.

3. Challenge educational orthodoxies in the best interests of achieving excellence, harnessing the findings of well-evidenced research to frame self-regulating and self-improving schools.

4. Shape the current and future quality of the teaching profession through high quality training and sustained professional development for all staff.

5. Model entrepreneurial and innovative approaches to school improvement, leadership and governance, confident of the vital contribution of internal and external accountability.

6. Inspire and influence others – within and beyond schools – to believe in the fundamental importance of education in young people's lives and to promote the value of education.

Department for Education (2015) National standards of excellence for headteachers. London: The Stationery Office. Retrieved from: www.bit.ly/2t5n9GI

Appendix 7

Getting the simple things right: Charlie Taylor's behaviour checklists

Key principles for headteachers to help improve school behaviour:

Policy

Ensure absolute clarity about the expected standard of pupils' behaviour.

Ensure that behaviour policy is clearly understood by all staff, parents and pupils.

Display school rules clearly in classes and around the building. Staff and pupils should know what they are.

Display the tariff of sanctions and rewards in each class.

Have a system in place for ensuring that children never miss out on sanctions or rewards.

Leadership

Model the behaviour you want to see from your staff.

Building

Visit the lunch hall and playground, and be around at the beginning and the end of the school day.

Ensure that other SLT members are a visible presence around the school.

Check that pupils come in from the playground and move around the school in an orderly manner.

Check up on behaviour outside the school.

Check the building is clean and well maintained.

Staff

Know the names of all staff.

Praise the good performance of staff.

Take action to deal with poor teaching or staff who fail to follow the behaviour policy.

Children

Praise good behaviour.

Celebrate successes.

Teaching

Monitor the amount of praise, rewards and punishments given by individual staff.

Ensure that staff praise good behaviour and work.

Ensure that staff understand special needs of pupils.

Individual pupils

Have clear plans for pupils likely to misbehave and ensure staff are aware of them.

Put in place suitable support for pupils with behavioural difficulties.

Parents

Build positive relationships with the parents of pupils with behaviour difficulties.

Behaviour checklist for teachers:

Classroom

Know the names and roles of any adults in class.

Meet and greet pupils when they come into the classroom.

Display rules in the class – and ensure that the pupils and staff know what they are.

Display the tariff of sanctions in class.

Have a system in place to follow through with all sanctions.

Display the tariff of rewards in class.

Have a system in place to follow through with all rewards.

Have a visual timetable on the wall.

Follow the school behaviour policy.

Pupils

Know the names of children.

Have a plan for children who are likely to misbehave.

Ensure other adults in the class know the plan.

Understand pupils' special needs.

Teaching

Ensure that all resources are prepared in advance.

Praise the behaviour you want to see more of.

Praise children doing the right thing more than criticising those who are doing the wrong thing (parallel praise).

Differentiate.

Stay calm.

Have clear routines for transitions and for stopping the class.

Teach children the class routines.

Parents

Give feedback to parents about their child's behaviour – let them know about the good days as well as the bad ones.

Taylor, C. (2011) Getting the simple things right: Charlie Taylor's behaviour checklists. Department for Education. London: The Stationery Office. Retrieved from: www.bit.ly/2QfGkLw

Appendix 8
School improvement plan on a page

Quality of education

Leadership and management

Term 1

Term 1

Term 2

Term 2

Term 3

Term 3

Term 3

Term 3

Term 2

Term 2

Term 1

Term 1

Personal development

Behaviour and attitudes

Appendix 9
How do you feel?

disappointed	puzzled	happy	confident
guilty	indifferent	determined	optimistic
frustrated	apologetic	concentrating	interested
disgusted	bored	relieved	content
lonely	undecided	satisfied	thoughtful
miserable	sad	surprised	relaxed
exhausted	anxious	hot	ecstatic

HOW DO YOU FEEL?

CPSIA information can be obtained
at www.ICGtesting.com
Printed in the USA
JSHW012253020220
3953JS00005B/7